MORE PRAISE FOR *BEFRIENDING*

"Arnie is an educator of extraordinary depth. This is in part because he lives 'the examined life' and has the touch to enable others—friends, colleagues, students, clients, restaurant owners—to do the same. This humble man is a very talented person who, with his unusually active mind, soul, and body, keeps as all at it—e.g., at life."

—Dr. Robert "Bob" C. Kimball (1928–2017), dean and professor of theology, author and editor of numerous books, and literary executor to the estate of Paul Tillich

"Reading it was much like sharing stories over a good meal, nuggets of wisdom surfacing throughout!"

—Sister Mary Ann Farley, spiritual director

"Although clearly structured, it's loose, and it pirouettes between the deep, raw personal and the didactic old rebbe."

—Paul Bailey, former president of the New Zealand Psychotherapy Association

"Befriending Your Stranger is a cogent and reliable guide for your journey of healing. It is a wise and well-written handbook for clearing emotional baggage and setting a baseline for balance and equanimity. Arnie covers a lot of spiritual territory, and he shares not just his story and roots but what he learned on his own journey. It's not so much that his messages are new as that they are framed in an invitational, compassionate voice. The meditations and exercises are interesting and useful, and they come the way a comma might in a sentence: to offer respite and a chance to integrate. It's like making a great new friend, and that friend is you. This is not a book to be swallowed. As Arnie would say, take a breath. Then settle in to do the work that your soul is asking you to do. Your Stranger will be a stranger no more."

—Helen Rosenau, author of *The Messy Joys of Being Human*

BEFRIENDING YOUR STRANGER

Befriending Your Stranger

AN ACTIVE JOURNEY TO INNER JOY

Arnie Freiman

SOPHUS
PRESS

SOPHUS
PRESS

Sophus Press
www.sophuspress.com
info@sophuspress.com
(727) 280-6295

Book design by Brad Grigor, Turning Point Arts
Cover by Flipside Creative
Author photograph by Margaret Wright Photography

Print ISBN: 978-1-7336739-0-7
ePUB ISBN: 978-1-7336739-1-4
Kindle ISBN: 978-1-7336739-2-1

For information about booking the author for an event, please contact:
Arnie Freiman
arniefreiman.com
arnie@arniefreiman.com

PRINTED IN CANADA

To those on a walk, an elusive journey, guided by inner listening.
To those who offered their heart and mind,
as well as others who saw an open heart to shape into their image.
May we find our way to bring ourselves fully into our story.

Invitation to Healing

The only reason we don't open our hearts and minds to other people is that they trigger confusion in us that we don't feel brave enough or sane enough to deal with. To the degree that we look clearly and compassionately at ourselves, we feel confident and fearless about looking into someone else's eyes.

PEMA CHÖDRÖN

LET'S TAKE A JOURNEY.

Hello, I'm Arnie, and I want to introduce you to your Stranger.

Who is your Stranger? Your Stranger is your truest self. And befriending your Stranger is a complex and dynamic journey of fully mining the deep connections that define us. So many of us, while looking for what makes us feel happy, safe, and balanced, spend our time anxiously fixated on a cycle of questions we don't understand. And that is because we've been taught to look for health and happiness in the wrong places. This toxic pattern is a by-product of a consumer-based society that wants to condition you to view yourself as a commodity. You are *not* a commodity. You are a miracle. I want to teach you how to look in the right places for your true center and befriend your Stranger.

We all carry the scars of painful experiences; those scars lie within us, where we can't see them easily. Often the pain is so great that we have an urge to resist seeing it at all or understanding its root causes, and so we are also unable to see a path beyond that pain. Our egos insulate us and attempt to protect us from the things in our lives that require the most immediate attention—such as healing our inner wounds. We live in a culture designed to distract us from our own greatness and larger purpose. I'm here to help you see beyond the distractions and discover who you were before your mind was invaded by a false narrative.

I know that everyone has an internal code of core beliefs and values. This code is different for every person. Unfortunately, many of us have lost the ability to see and hear our own codes. We need to relearn how to approach ourselves, examine our inner values, and reevaluate our connection with the world. This form of deeper listening empowers us to be receptive to that guiding spirit within each of us. I can guide you into a new relationship and a new dynamic with yourself—with your Stranger—which will enable you to heal.

So, I invite you to take a healing journey with me. This is likely not the first healing journey you've undertaken. Writing this book has been one of many healing journeys for me as well. Throughout this guide, I relay some of my personal experiences with healing, and I hope they parallel and enrich your journey. My hope is that these anecdotes will help you more fully understand the concepts in this book as I introduce you to new paths of perception and new tools for living, designed to guide you on your own pathway to health and happiness. I look forward to being a part of that very special journey.

WHO AM I?

Let me introduce myself. I hold a PhD, MDiv, MEd, and a CFP. But mainly, I'm Arnie, a mensch from New York, and I'm here to help. I'm not going to beat around the bush with you or waste your time. Life has beaten me down once or twice, but it has also cracked me up. I have dealt with cancer, loss, pain, divorce, and the worst kinds of existential ennui. I continue to have a turbulent struggle with many aspects of our culture. However, instead of succumbing to these conditions, I chose a path of healing. Sometimes I didn't know if I would ever recover, but I persisted. I couple my determination with studies in academia, theology, natural healing, and community from a variety of schools and cultures.

In my work life, I created and designed community-based internship programs. I was one of the earliest people to introduce holistic health education in a major American university, and I cofounded the first school of acupuncture in the country. Later, I also founded the first school of naturopathic medicine in the state of California. Ultimately, I survived the bad and met the good because I learned how to return to my center and find my balance—as I want to help you do.

I became an activist for accessible health care and organized empowered healing communities across America. I've filled my life with deep self-work, academic pursuits, natural healing, world travel, and inspiration. I've befriended and debated with some of the greatest philosophical minds of our times.

All of my searching has led me to this profound truth: *true* healing is about connection—and the first connection you must make is with yourself. I want to help you discover and embrace your Stranger. Wisdom echoes within all of us, but we need to relearn how to access it. You won't find truth on TV. Real answers can't be defrosted and microwaved. The key of this journey is learning to reconnect to parts of yourself that have become numbed or muted, thereby restoring balance to your life. We can't accomplish that task successfully in isolation. Healing comes from transformative reconnection—with ourselves, with others, and with the Divine. Now, the "Divine" goes by many different names (God, Mother Earth, universal knowledge, the sacred, and so on) and can mean many things to different people. Here I'm using it as a general spiritual term. The Divine in this book is *your* specific belief system, whatever that may be.

The point is that healing is not an "I" journey. It's an "I-Thou" path—a demanding, renewing, and rewarding pilgrimage of discovery. As I said, this book is one of many journeys for me, and I'm better than ever! More importantly, you can be, too.

HOW TO USE THIS BOOK

Our psychic foundations are complex, built over time by many different experiences and influences—some constructive and some not. In order to reset harmful thinking patterns, you have to engage in compartmentalized self-examination of each crucial part of yourself before moving on; in other words, you will need to rebuild from the bottom up. Once you grow into a deeper understanding and connection with yourself and your more foundational motivations, you can find freedom from what has been dragging you down.

Through years of study, travel, trial, error, and connection, I have come up with a fluid process to help you rediscover and rebuild your foundations. This process can be summed up in the Eight Qualities of the Heart listed below. If you will notice, these qualities are all action words—and that's because inner healing requires hard work.

It requires you to *act*. However, by first *practicing* these qualities, you will awaken an inner balance, drive, and intuition that is buried and silenced in so many of us.

EIGHT QUALITIES OF THE HEART

RECLAIMING	Turning down the volume of the false messages you've received in life to identify your own truth
PROCLAIMING	Making space for your truth in the world
OPENING	Making space for the world in yourself
LISTENING	Learning to connect with others in healthy ways free of defensiveness or judgment
UNITING	Connecting with the Divine within yourself and turning that connection into meaningful action
MEETING	Greeting the ancient wisdom within you fully
BEFRIENDING	Manifesting the wisdom you have learned as action
APPRECIATING	Manifesting gratitude to the divine kernel of love that keeps you going beyond your breakthrough; shifting your reality to create a solid home for yourself

As we go through each quality and each chapter, I will introduce you to some philosophical content, which I will pair with stories from my own life that help illustrate the main points. At the end of each chapter, I have included a practice portion with exercises that will help you implement these philosophies in your own life.

I have also punctuated each section of the journey with inspirational poetry that came to me through utilizing this process. I hope these poems will speak to the part of yourself in need of healing. These dynamic offerings are intended to galvanize your growth and further you on your unique path to authenticity, inner balance, and harmony.

Ultimately, your Stranger is YOU. But a transformed you, free from certain bonds of your own invention that were first cultivated by a predatory society. Your Stranger is also your connection beyond yourself—a clear you, rooted in your own authenticity, fused through a deep connectivity with life, divinity, community, and the inner child who has always been calling out from the other side of doubt, bad patterns, and anxiety.

When you befriend your Stranger, false walls come down, and you gain new clarity. This will help you find the freedom to build and live your best life. Health and happiness—that's what you are looking for and that's what you deserve. But you have to earn it! I want to help you achieve that seemingly elusive goal. I hope this book will be a valuable tool to use over and over again to refocus and empower you on your unique healing journey. Let's get started!

CHAPTER ONE

Reclaiming

He not busy being born is busy dying.

BOB DYLAN

RECLAIM

Take me into the Divine Mystery
Of Life.
I am in search of my Soul,
Looking for that place
Of Wholeness
Where healing is at home
And we come to be in the One.
I hear tell God resides there,
And the way in is through Love.
Help me to come through my fear
And enter into the garden of wonder and awe.
Amen.

BEFORE WE CAN EXPECT TO HEAL AND BE WHOLE, AND BEFORE WE can learn to meet our Stranger, we must be fully present. In this chapter, I am calling on you to reclaim your birthright to belong—to yourself, to your fellow human beings, and to the One Source. In this belonging is healing. To "reclaim" is to revisit with new perspective the events, relationships, and stories that brought you to this moment. Raising consciousness, resting, and contemplating are the revolutionary acts of today. Together they constitute the process of reclamation, which is very important because it is the first step toward healing. That's why you're here.

The first part of reclaiming ourselves is to examine how we listen and what we listen to. Each of us is driven by strong personal and societal motives. We move through life as if it were a furnace stoked by ambition. We are constantly moving; it is part of our nature. In proper proportion, this inner drive is a healthy part of who we are. But where is that path taking us? What is its focal point? We take our motivations for granted, but in reality, we build them brick by brick. And amidst the enormous force of the external world to claim and conquer ground, we often forget that the greatest wilderness we are provided exists within.

Who are *you*? When you plant those flags on the things you conquer in your life, what do those banners stand for? How does this complex, beautiful, and infinite being you are differ from the person you have spent your life being *told* that you are? What can you learn about yourself, through honest, present reflection, that might represent a shift from false narratives that were pitched long ago to you and are now trapping you in their irrelevance and toxic messages?

The lifelong cycle begins before we're old enough to process and interpret the input we receive, directly and indirectly, from the world around us. Navigating through all of these external voices until you can hear your Stranger's voice is an odyssey, and when you set out to do this, burrowing within to lose all the other voices so that you can listen to your own is the first pivotal moment in reclaiming your own identity.

Before we move further into theory, I'd like to offer you some of my own story, gathered through conscious contemplation, as a way to spark your own reclamation. Among other things, I wish to illustrate a basic truth: many of us view our identities as fixed, rigid, and inherent, but in reality, our identities are malleable. The truest path to ourselves is attained through what I call "directed fluidity." In other words, we must relearn to be open and aware to the lessons life continually offers us.

I struggled to reclaim my own story for many years. I was raised in an American Jewish Modern Orthodox home in Far Rockaway, New York. Each day, after attending public school, I went to Hebrew school. It was a taxing schedule for a child. In addition to the long weekdays, I spent each Saturday and many evenings with the elders. Our elders required a minimum of ten men to hold communal prayer, and so I, a young man in the eyes of our culture, joined them.

Even in the welcoming of the faith and warmth of the community, I had questions. I began to feel my own story begin to form and resonate within my consciousness, but it was stifled. I struggled as the words of the authority figures in my community effortlessly took center stage and dominated my emerging perspective, even though they were supposedly talking about *me*. When we are young, we are like fledglings seeking direction, and we are at our most vulnerable. That is when we begin to become our own Stranger and start down the long path of estrangement from the natural world. And the voices of others begin to override our own instincts regarding our own nature. For many of us, our youth is also the period when we are the *most* awake to deeper truths, but of course we don't realize it.

To understand directed fluidity, first we must try to strip away the lenses we have been taught to use to see ourselves. So much of what we view as our identity, and which we take as fundamental reality, is our subjective perception, filtered and manipulated by the lenses through which we view the world and ourselves in relation to it. Our personal stories are thus supplanted by the vicarious experiences of others at the expense of our own growth.

What exists beyond those walls we have built? Is it freedom? Is it peace? Is it just a more real version of ourselves? You'll never know until you learn how to look beyond the walls. How do we look past this programming and learn to see ourselves with clarity? We may never know how many colors exist in the world because we only know the limits of what our own eyes can perceive, and by the terms others have given them. Science gives us tools to realize there is a much broader spectrum. Soul gives us the ability to see ourselves with new depth. We need tools to see in a new way.

Each culture and time has its own perspective and put its own stamp on divine revelation, and indoctrination starts early. What makes some words holy and others subjective? Are holy words the ones written in a special book, sung by an ordained cantor or choir, or spoken by teachers and friends? What about the words, thoughts, and inclinations percolating, in sincerity, within each of us? How do they face off against the stone-carved creeds of dogma? Do we need them all? Do we need them *at* all?

As I grew in my relation to the world, I sometimes felt the words and voices of others were surrounding me and binding me far too tightly. When I left Far Rockaway for college in Washington, DC, the Vietnam War was raging, and the draft was in full swing. Being in college during the sixties and seventies was, in general, exhilarating and tumultuous. I struggled, with little self-awareness, because development of a deeper sense of self was given little encouragement at home. I fumbled and flailed awkwardly, and my soft, vulnerable side made an appearance only when wrapped around emotional outbursts of identity confusion.

"Business" was a dirty word to a sensitive, politically correct, anti-war activist, so I ran past the Business School building every day and pushed down my natural entrepreneurial skills. There were so many ghosts haunting my inner story of self, because I wanted to be the good boy, microcosmically pleasing to my immediate family, my culture, and the communities and cultures I was fashioned by, during a period when so many of the conventional definitions of previous generations had become fluid and were being radically shaken up, giving birth to the sensitive male and the politically correct young man.

Where was I to find my teachers and guides? With my draft lottery number coming due, I went to my rabbi, who had been my family's guide and spiritual leader for a lifetime. He had been the well of wisdom in my life up to that point. I asked him to write a letter in support of my application for conscientious objector status. He refused. And, in short order, my father also refused to draft a letter on my behalf.

This signaled the beginning of a conflict of paradigms within me. As the venerable monk Thich Nhat Hanh said, "At any moment, you have a choice that either leads you closer to your spirit or further away from it." These men, and my own inner voice, had long cultivated what I thought were my deepest values. Now those voices were at odds, and the two most important men in my life up to that point would not hear what my heart wanted to say.

To me, my opposition to the actions in Vietnam was not in spite of my Jewish faith, but due to it. I asked my father to write a letter even if he disagreed with me, but he refused. He was telling me to be quiet, to silence my own voice and defer to his. I understood his perspective. He felt that the United States was a great country to fit into—if we were quiet. The past had punished the Jewish people for our voices. Dad suggested joining the National Guard to avoid combat. That wasn't me. I wasn't running from a fight; I was pursuing my own path toward integrity in this life. There would be no National Guard. No medical deferment, nor self-injury; no flight to Canada. I was a Jew. I was an American. I was a student of the prophet Micah. I would not be quiet. I would stand my ground and speak my truth: war isn't the way to solve conflict!

Ultimately, because of the refusal of the rabbi and my father, and because of my own decision not to stand down, I began my search for authenticity outside Judaism. I knew I needed new voices that didn't require me to suppress my own. I sought the support of draft counselors and was introduced to the American Friends Service Committee, a Quaker peace and justice group organized by folks in the peace community. In their practice, they honed themselves and their relation to the Divine through hours upon hours of Zen-like silence, openness, and contemplation in an almost surgically sterile environment. It was initially both overwhelming and culturally shocking. For the first time, I stepped out of the constant kinetic verbiage of a synagogue that had ultimately sought to silence me. And in the quiet of the Quaker message, I better learned how to listen to a voice within. Finally, through exploring this new tradition of silence, I was finding myself heard.

So, I had been presented with an opportunity to choose. It's important to learn how to see *choice* in reclaiming your life. For me, the stakes were high. If I clung exclusively to the comfort of the hierarchical views of my own culture, I would have had to sacrifice integral elements of my own truth. So, I chose to attempt to grow beyond those walls.

In reclaiming ourselves, it's important to find a community that supports us in aligning ourselves with our own story. The Quakers made space for me to be a conscientious objector, to honor myself, and to accept my own voice—acts essential to healing.

It was a busy, confusing time to be finding oneself, especially considering that the American marketplace ideals of "self" possibly didn't exist anyway. Eastern spiritual teachings were extolling the death of the self as they proclaimed that we are one and that the individual self is an illusion. In the times of personal searching, I continued to misplace my "self" often, only to glimpse it again on the path, a little farther down.

From cradle to grave, much of who we are is dictated to us, as well who we should be, what we should believe, and what path we should take. Culture is a valuable and, of course, inextricable part of who we are. But we remain responsible for staying behind the wheel of our own lives. And we are each blessed with our own unique voice, compass, and choices. If you are always being the "good boy" or "good girl," putting on the face of who society deems you should be, are you wearing your true face or a mask designed by others? Would you even recognize yourself outside of the context of your life? Ultimately, that is the key question when identifying your own soul. The risk in strictly adhering to the path laid out by others is that *you* may become lost in the process. You begin to split, and part of you becomes a Stranger. If we have faith only in the knowledge offered by others, we miss the wisdom forged by the experiences leading to that knowledge, and we miss the potential that we may come to different conclusions.

Don't live life on autopilot as I did in my youth. Nor would it be wise to bite at every hook that shimmers before you. We waste a lot of time batting ourselves back and forth between the logical fallacy of alternating extremes. Things like a war, in my case Vietnam, are polarizing moments. While I wanted to protest the conflict itself, I wanted to do so with love in my heart. So many marches for peace were filled with the same vitriol and anger I stood against, rather than with the heart I sought. I am reminded of a story told by Thich Nhat Hanh about the American peace community. He observed that they were skillful at marching and fighting against war, but they struggled with knowing how to love and be gentle with one another or, as I would put it, befriending the Stranger. This comes from balance—and I still hadn't found it.

My journey continued, both in the college classroom and far beyond it. As I journeyed, I sought balance. With the spiritual support of the Quaker community, I continued to pursue depth, cultivate the light within me, and act according to my evolving sense of community. However, this pursuit was not at the expense of my cultural identity of being Jewish or my father's son. In reality, this choice enabled me to live up to the promise of the greater values of faith and courage instilled in me. While in college, I founded an organization devoted to social change and activism that also promoted a student-run business model, and I started to home in on my path.

Immediately after graduation, a consulting firm recruited me, but the innovative idea I had for a cluster college model was lost to in-fighting in the firm. For me, this became a very real experience in the world of subtle betrayal—a theme that would be repeated a number of times in my lifetime of learning and growing. More to the point, I once again felt muted. Ultimately, I pointed my wagon toward West Virginia, where I became involved with a community college. This gave me the opportunity to listen deeply to what a community needed. But when I tried to offer programs that fulfilled those needs, I was shut down by the institution and local government that wanted to keep things how they already were. They weren't hearing the voice of the new generation, and that wasn't a good strategy in such radical times.

As my chapter in West Virginia ended, new possibilities were born. I met and fell in love with my first wife and accepted a doctoral fellowship in higher education at the University of Massachusetts Amherst. They provided funds, an office, and support to design integrative learning models for one of the first programs in holistic health care in a major university. I also met Werner, a retired surgeon and a student of theosophy. Remaining fluid yet committed to my path was serving me vocationally and bolstering my inner growth. It was also making me more critical of arbitrary acceptance of the system, and I was able to see the higher potential of what that system could become. The next chapters of my life, in the seventies, were brisk and galvanizing, like an ocean journey of exploration.

I started work with Werner in the lab he'd been given at the university, and I studied and experimented with various modalities of healing, including acupuncture. I pursued this development in innovative medicine and health care with great enthusiasm. Through acupuncture, I learned about the power inherent in a health care system that looks at the entire human living within a complex environment.

This insight, in turn, extended into my family life. My wife wasn't able to conceive—at least, that was the view shared by Western practitioners. Yet we experimented with acupuncture, and she became pregnant! Hearing a deeper voice, we had wanted to try something outside of the traditional system. I became so impressed with a health care system that engaged all the elements of life, I became a student of Eastern philosophy and medicine while still working on my doctorate.

From 1973 to 1975, I worked with Dr. Tin Yau So to open the New England School of Acupuncture, the first licensed school of acupuncture in the United States. I became so involved with Chinese medicine that I finally dropped the doctoral program and accepted a master's degree in education. I had found some peace within my turbulent sea and was enthusiastic about delving deeply into the ancient and esoteric truths of other cultures and beyond the institutions that had previously framed my path.

In 1979 we went west and migrated to Northern California, where I furthered my studies in natural medicine and philosophy. I was inspired and spent two years working feverishly to open the Pacific College of Naturopathic Medicine in the Russian River area. It was a heady battle. One thing we must always keep in mind is that our truths are not always shared by all. The school was a challenge to bring to fruition and even more difficult to operate. Securing licensure was another battle I fought, yet the faculty and students paid little attention. The opposition was deflating. Personality conflicts and ego among the diverse students, faculty, and administration of the school were so severe that I was forced to leave. The school didn't last much longer, even with the foundational support in place.

Physically and emotionally depleted from the closure of my school, I was now sick in both body and spirit. Then I was diagnosed with Hodgkin's lymphoma.

But purpose will continue to reveal itself if we don't solely rely upon circumstance to define our reality. Sitting in the basement of Stanford Medical Center in the day treatment center for oncology patients, I encountered the ultimate irony of my life so far. Here I was confronted with the opposite of what a health-based, nurturing environment should be. This was a health care facility for people facing life-threatening illnesses, yet there were no windows, little ventilation, uncomfortable chairs, and long waits. The stench of death was all around.

The oncologists would respond only to issues that they felt directly related to Hodgkin's disease. Therefore, my gaining one hundred pounds was a matter for Weight Watchers. Family issues and trauma were for social workers. Job-related matters were for the vocational counselors. Matters of the heart and spirit were for the chaplains. Much like the rest of life in this society, it was a marginalizing and fragmented divide-and-conquer philosophy incongruently designed to confront a challenge where healing was only possible through attaining total synergistic balance. I was dumbstruck.

Surprisingly, thrown into this controlled "*un*healing" energy of fighting cancer in my system, I was told that I was lucky I was so healthy. That cultivated modern system had resorted to appealing to the chaos of luck. At that moment, my whole being realized that I would need to find my own place of balance and maintain a healing light within, or I wouldn't make it. Learning how and what to ask the appropriate player was a vital part of my healing process. Obviously, for me, as someone who had studied and practiced Chinese, naturo-pathic, and chiropractic medicine—which see the whole person as part of an integrated environment—this challenge was of vital importance.

Ultimately, I chose a Doctor of Chinese Medicine, who happened to be a Jewish man who came into this life with a Chinese-ancestor soul, to serve as the conductor of this discordant ensemble of health care providers. The solution to imbalance is not conflict but equilibrium. I was the horse caught in the barbed-wire fence. The solution to my chaos was not struggle but rather learning to discern the right kind of help. Once I reclaimed my health choices, I started to get healthy.

But that was only one battle I fought. I needed work, and the only work that could offer me health insurance without a "preexisting condition" clause and simultaneously afford the opportunity to make enough money to maintain my home and family while expending limited energy was selling cars. This was survival mode. To my dis-belief, I became one of the most successful salespeople on the West Coast and was offered my own dealership in an industry I both despised and knew little about.

This was, by all respects, the lowest point of my life. I had cancer, as well as two babies, a wife, and a home to support as sole breadwin-ner. I was carrying the weight of deep professional disappointment and low self-esteem. I was depressed, and I felt disconnected from my own life and from my "self." But life goes on, especially when we're fighting to survive. So, how do we sustain ourselves during periods when the external components of our lives appear to be out of control?

Besides dealing with sustaining the mortal coil, I found that I was also becoming angry. I felt failed by our system in many ways, a mentality our culture seems to be embracing. But anger can be powerfully motivating, if we don't wallow. Through my own process, I grew so knowledgeable about the labyrinth of modern health insurance that I acted as a volunteer consultant for various service groups. After doing this for a few years, I turned my support into a business, and in 1985, Partners Financial Insurance Services was born. My reclamation and restoration had begun.

During this time, about two-thirds of the way through cancer treatments, I was besieged with questions about the human experience, such as: What do I really want to do, for me? What would touch my heart and open my soul? Psychology had no answers for such primal questions, and I felt called to revisit a forgotten desire to attend seminary. I was going through the process of reclamation yet again. That's something to note. It never stops; we never stop growing, shifting, and needing to listen to ourselves to honor that direction. In honor of the direction *my* life traveled, instead of studying to become a rabbi, I enrolled at Starr King School within the Graduate Theological Union in Berkeley.

The Unitarian church has a tradition of cultivating big hearts and minds, and seminary was where I was most at home. I was inspired by the modern Unitarian movement and by philosophical writers and thinkers such as Ralph Waldo Emerson, Henry David Thoreau, and other Transcendentalists. Intense study of these philosophers, who often cultivated their explorations through artistic testimony, would connect laterally to other seeds within me and come to fruition later on. We will get into that later. Back then, I was seeing various roads in my life come together in a broader sense; I was enlivened by the belief that our social action has to come out of a deeper, latent essence. For me, that essence is the deep well of the sacred well within me. I was authenticating and unifying my values through practice. I was learning to listen. If it had been possible, I never would have left the seminary. What a candy store for someone like me!

How do we learn to listen? We practice. My need for simple connection with the Divine became apparent to me in 1993, right after seminary, when I entered a program called Clinical Pastoral Education. In this intensive full-time position, I worked as a clinical hospital chaplain. I would enter rooms at one of the most primal stages in the lives of individuals and their families. I found that many people wanted to share their stories with someone. I learned that chaplains can walk into a room with their own definition of who these people are, or they can approach as a receptive, listening presence. The latter means sometimes listening for the unspoken words.

One day at the hospital, I walked into the room of an elderly man, accompanied by my colleague, a Catholic chaplain. The man was in bed, drawing the very last breaths of life, surrounded by his family, including his wife, children, grandchildren, and great-grandchildren. Surrounded by generations of his lineage, he was clinging to life, and as we spent time with his family, we both noticed that a deep, palpable love filled the space around him.

My colleague requested to take the lead, and she asked his wife to walk outside the room for a moment with us. Taking the woman's hand, she said, "He needs you to assure him you're all going to be fine and that the time is good for him to rest."

When we all returned to the room, the man's wife offered that assurance to her husband. Then, while holding hands and looking into each other's eyes, he died into healing.

That day, I learned a powerful lesson in the gifts of deep listening. Once we learn to listen to what others need but struggle to say, we can learn to listen to that quiet, persistent voice that we often mute within ourselves.

When my chaplaincy concluded, I thought I would finally have time to refocus on the basics in my life and deepen my connection with my wife. We'd been married for twenty-four years and our girls were off to college. We went to Santa Fe to celebrate our anniversary.

I felt that we had the possibility of sharing in a solid partnership after a long and hard journey. On the eve of our anniversary, I shared that I needed to grieve for my cancer, to allow the river of pain and sorrow to flow out of me. I asked if I could do that now with her help. She said yes, but the next morning when we returned home, she told me she wanted a divorce, and she soon moved out of our house.

Now I was beyond anger; I was numb. I felt the abandonment and betrayal so acutely that it overwhelmed my ability to function. On a core level, I was having an identity crisis of a different nature. For almost a quarter of a century, I had had a clear role as a husband and provider! I survived, in part, to remain in that role. What did I have now? After winning what had been the biggest battle of my life up to that point, I heard chaos calling again to me from the wild.

Among other things, the urge to write first surfaced during this period. The poems I shared in the first pages of this book were from this time, when I needed to heal from the wounds of betrayal. When I finally answered that calling and put pen to paper, a new kind of healing began. It was almost a prayer in reverse—I was translating the answers I had sought, not unlike some of my own influences. We'll come back to this idea of writing and translation as a tool for healing.

I also drew heavily on the wisdom budding from a friendship that had begun several years before, as I studied the seminary. For three and a half years, from 1988 to 1991, in between treatments and taking care of family and clients, I was granted the right to explore the depths of human inquiry with some of the greatest hearts and minds of the era. Among them was a man named Bob, a great Unitarian theologian.

Bob was a rare man who lived in his place of truth and integrity and therefore who struck fear in the hearts of students. Having a strong personality myself, I had a strong desire to meet him, but at that time, Bob was no longer teaching group classes. He only did one-on-one tutorials. The first time I met him, he lived up to his reputation and asked me to leave his office immediately.

But before I got too far, something in me made me want to run back. What was it? I felt there was real rigor to this man, and I wanted to know more about it. Yes, he'd triggered me, but I ultimately honored my deeper instinct not to run away from him. Instead I chose to stand up for what became one of the most profound relationships in my life. I came to realize that, in the tradition of the old ways, he wasn't rejecting me but rather testing my resolve. My return illustrated my desire to learn beyond my own ego, as I strode back to his office and through his door, proclaiming, "No. You and I are going to do some work together."

"Well, then, sit down," he said.

Bob was a cosmic trickster, and we never stopped our work together. He became my guide in seminary and in further exploring the Transcendentalists and great sacred poets—Emerson, Fuller, Hawthorne, and Melville. As I studied the great thinkers of lands far and near, I felt the presence of something special. Thus, Bob invited me and his other students to regain our own authenticity. In life, if we listen, we will find ways to plant and cultivate the seeds within us. If you persistently pursue your own authenticity, you might find yourself surprised one day at how much strength you have amassed in dormancy. As you think about reclaiming your past, try to remember those strong voices that bolstered and uplifted your own.

In addition to these additional wise voices, during my studies I met with the words of Martin Buber and Rabbi Abraham Joshua Heschel. As a child, the synagogue had been the centerpiece of our home and neighborhood, including our rabbi, who lived around the corner. For years I went to Hebrew school daily and to Saturday morning services. Yet, with all that Jewish pedagogy, I'd never heard the names of Buber and Heschel, the two most pivotal Jewish voices of the twentieth century.

It took coming to the largest partnership of seminaries and graduate schools in the United States to engage in their heart-centered teachings. Bob and I delved into their teachings on the depth of the relational and heart-centered prayer. For years, as he became more familiar with me and my past, Bob would exclaim with a smile, "Arnie, Martin Buber is a Jew!"

Toward the end of his calling as teacher of religious leadership, Bob believed he was complicit with violence to the students' minds by telling them anything at all and stepped down from the class-room lectern to sit down, with crayons and a writing pad, beside his students.

A question loomed—how do we move from a place of constantly being told to a place of paying attention? How does love enter the room as an honored member of our circle? And how do we invite the sacred into our discourse? Bob chose to illustrate this by using a green crayon to teach about openness and a purple crayon to teach about cautionary cutting. He'd sit beside me as we colored. All of us came to the room prepared to meet each other with our fears and joys.

During my time in seminary, I searched for meaning, which took on the shape of something much deeper and beyond the self. Being raised Jewish, conversation about Jesus did not happen in our home or center of religious education and worship. It was as though the New Testament did not exist. So, looking at the man Saul, who during a journey fell off his horse and awoke as Paul, was a new and profound experience. He felt he heard the voice of Jesus. But that was *his* listening. That was *his* story.

How does that go from being his story to being the story of millions of people who frame it and define how it will govern the lives of nations and families? The story possibly worked for Paul, and may have worked for others along the way, but what does that have to do with *my* hearing? And where is the love, if that is what we are so concerned about? I related to Saul, because I wanted to understand why there were mountains to climb and such long waits for the word of God to come down. That, too, became a part of my journey.

Of course, surviving cancer and enduring divorce are not the end of my story. Our stories are never really over, despite these moments where we are forced to start anew. After the divorce, I purged my belongings, moved north to Oregon, married again, moved to New Zealand and Tasmania, and divorced again. What followed was a perpetually reimagined work life, more healing, new friendships, and a continued cultivation of the relationships that sustain me.

Our lives are a dance of brokenness and a return to wholeness. The dance articulates its many steps in the ways we connect with other humans and as humans within institutions. And the dance continues, in the ways we disconnect and forget ourselves and yearn to belong, and in how we learn to return home and reclaim ourselves.

Even after I'd left seminary studies, Bob and I continued to sit in various Indian restaurants whenever I was in Berkeley for over twenty years. We started with the question, "Do humans have the capacity to live an institutional life without doing violence to one another?" And this is a theme that would recur in my life: in faith, in culture, in health, in marriage. But the real topic was always our enduring friendship, the meeting point of two men agreeing to commit to one another and the integrity of our bond.

Take Martin Buber, another of the great thinkers who inspire me. Buber helps us understand that the sacred does not live in an edifice, a text, or the mouth of a motivating person. The sacred comes from meeting. For meeting to take place, Buber concluded that it took the recognition of a clearly identified center, strong and real enough to hold the spokes of our lives. It takes surrender. And in surrendering to the center—a center that is neither ourselves nor an object but something deeper, both within and beyond ourselves—we continue coming into and through creation.

One of the sad by-products of the alienation caused by losing our connection is institutionalized law, or as Bob called it, "the category of things as the dominant role in society." Law makes things simple: there is a proper way and a way that is not proper. Law was behind my father and my rabbi when they refused to support me as a conscientious objector. Law disrupted the education of a community I was trying to serve. Law prevented the licensure of much-needed health care. Law can often silence and sterilize what could be fertile connection.

The issue is that we *want* to talk with one another. We want to touch one another, and we want to listen to and possibly challenge one another. We can rewrite an isolationist reaction to emotional and physical fear by coming together over a sense of deep love rather than violence. Bob believed that we have institutionalized isolation and that our culture chose law over love, forging our own imaginary fences around each of us, cemented by thousands of directives, all based on fear, intending to prevent us from deeply communing with one another. Ultimately, this system doesn't leave the soul much communion or companionship, or even a greater sense of meaning, to get through rough times.

If we cannot hear or feel each other, how can we learn to hear or feel ourselves? Isn't communication a blueprint for how we can hear beyond ourselves and ultimately perceive the messages offered by something greater?

Beyond the fear-based fences of what's unknown beyond ourselves, each of us is our own wilderness. That's exciting! When we were kids, we were connected. We believed the world could be anything we wanted. We loved fearlessly. Those were the tools we were given. Don't let your childhood be the high-water mark of your soul's development. Pick up and continue the work you started. Often, the greatest crises in our lives, the ones that get us up at night, are not the circumstantial tragedies but rather the existential ones, however they are articulated. And, by definition, if those answers exist, then they must be available. The charge remains ours to hone our ability to listen.

When we are distracted from listening and engaged in dogged, marketed pursuit of the base and corporeal terms of ego—identity and the simple delusion of safety—we feel the old dread and anxiety clawing at us to wake up. What are we so afraid of, and why do we create stories and institutions to codify and control our instincts? We become strangers to ourselves when we succumb to our fears, and that impedes us from identifying and pursuing the things in life that resonate most deeply within our souls. We become so afraid of losing or being injured during the race, we forget to run, or if we run, we hold back. We wear logos where we should be wearing our heart.

That's a hard truth to meet. I met it with great initial resistance, which is a natural response to having an unnatural reality shaken—comparable to shaking an addiction. So let's focus on what brought us here. Each of us wants to love and to take the time to care. We want to be whole and seen in a way that resonates within ourselves, in a way that calms us and makes us feel secure. Ultimately, that is the place of healing. But if we don't take the time and make the effort to meet and reclaim ourselves, then we end up leaving it to others to dictate and define ourselves for us. We forget how to really connect and be "in touch," and instead we just semi-engage in idle chitchat. We think skimming on the surface is safe and nonthreatening, but empty connection is exactly what the Transcendentalists (as just one example) didn't have time for. It adds to the well of anxiety because it causes us to disconnect. We push away the real truths and values we held when we weren't so afraid, and so we end up living inside the fear. That's a terrible way to live.

Our ancestors carved a place in this world for all of us. We must channel that spirit to grow beyond ourselves. Think of how much strength you could save by not fighting your fears but taming them and learning from them. Think of how your strength can, instead of going just toward your own survival, benefit the world we share. Then we'd walk into life fully, wholeheartedly, knowing we are all part of one shared life. The central prayer of Judaism, placed on doors, wrapped on our bodies, and sung in synagogue is, "*Shema Israel Adonai Elohenu Adonai Echad,*" which I translate as, "Listen, we are one."

———

The road, the sea, the journey—however you see your path in life—is never easy. The idea of the easy journey is an appeal to sentiment we get from commercials made by people trying to sell you something. Throughout my whole life, people tried to tell me who I was, what to think, how divine reality and law were already laid out for me and what my duties were to follow it. I felt like someone else's chess piece. And at each step, new voices arose to replace previous programming with new programming. And yet, the voice within persisted and dared me to follow it to its meaning. My identity and roles in life—of culture, of vocation, of marriage and geography—continue to shift. And yet I remain. You remain. And as we work together to move forward and find our truest selves, let me remind you that you have to trade the illusion of safety for the glory of peace—the peace that comes from knowing you have met yourself along the way, and you no longer have anything to hide.

PRACTICE

Over the next few pages, and throughout this book, I've included some of my poetry, which I wrote during my own reclamation process. I felt a deep calling to write, which forced me from my fixed place and filled me with something outside of me. I share it to complete the circuit, and I dare you to open yourselves to that deeper voice as well and see how it might choose to announce itself to you. Take a few moments to listen. What do you hear? After listening to my voice, listen to your own. Write down what comes to your mind. This practice will help you learn to identify your own voice among all the other voices competing for your attention. Look at your own life. Can you identify similar periods of conflict? What were the choices you were presented with? Did you realize you had a choice to make? To what outcomes did they lead? Did you move further or closer to reclaiming yourself?

The poems that follow were inspired by these and other questions and conflicts I encountered on my journey to befriend my Stranger. I hope they help you as you reflect on your own life.

GRADING MY LIFE

In the corners, the stuff resides.
I know because
It wells up and comes
Like waves smashing on the rocks
Of my tranquility.
So many pockets
The stuff can hide in
Till it's ready to appear—
Without announcement or invitation.
Emotions start flowing,
Demanding attention,
As though God were
Grading my life.

OPEN TO A SPACIOUSNESS

And so
The weights
Hold your feet
Down
So you can't grow
And move on.

Who are you kidding?
Just lift up your feet.
One at a time
Is just fine,
But not lifting
Even a toe
Keeps you planted
To the same time
And place
You said you want
To leave.

But it feels too heavy,
And the pain is
Too real.
Stay and be numb—
Or lift a toe,
Even for a moment,
And open to a spaciousness
You lost long ago.

SHAKE

Do you lie in bed
For those moments
Before you choose
To face the day,
When you begin
To feel you,
When you want
To run away from yourself?
Do you shake inside
With the turmoil
Of the ages
Coursing through your being?
When you feel all those
Years of who you
Really are,
Do you like it?
But you can't stop it.
You try to run,
Go to work, or play,
Only to have to return
To your bed once again
And again.
Who are you,
And can you
Make peace?
Can you love
Once again
As when you were fresh
And full of dreams?
For no matter when,
You will die.
There is only now,
And there is really only you.

WHERE ARE YOU?

To all of you
Who don't check in,
Where are you?
Do you wake at night
In turmoil or fear?
Do you allow the child to speak,
Or do you close it down
Abruptly or over time?
Do you remember listening
To your place of knowing,
Only to have Mom or Dad,
Teacher or neighbor
Or your best friend,
Tell you you're wrong?
Did it hurt too much
And you just wanted to
Be a member ... to belong?
Did you force it down
So that it's lost, or so
Deep down that the birth is too hard?
Introduce yourself to you—
Listen again for the first time.
I know it hurts deep,
But the loss is empty
With a life of no meaning.
Sooner or later and before death,
It hurts too deep to not be aware.

IN THE SILENCE

In the silence
Is when all the chatter occurs
When I am asked
To face the demons
Of my creation.
In the silence
I find the noise
At its loudest pitch,
Making little room
For the peaceful tone
To savor life.
In the silence
The wonder hides,
Afraid to show its face,
Full of surprise
For a journey lived.
In the silence
I still reach
For the memories
As though they are real today—
So here and now
Can't be felt, for
The sweet gift of life
In the moment
Of each creation.

BE GENTLE, BE TRUE

It's true, though,
That we hold
All too many ghosts
For years and
Lifetimes
We don't remember.
It feels so hard
When all we want
Is to be happy,
As fleeting as that is.
But the pain
Holds back the depth
Or puts us out
In the world
As heroes or successes,
Only to come back
And feel despair.
You can't run,
But we keep on trying
Until we see our face.
So be gentle
With yourself;
Be true,
And learn who you are.
Just allow time and space.
Give a gift to yourself
And start the work—
For it is work,
And yet joy—
To bring you to you.

CHAPTER TWO

Proclaiming

I knew who I was this morning,
but I've changed a few times since then.

LEWIS CARROLL

PROCLAIM

Born from the Divine,
Out of love
I proclaim
To belong to the
Community of the One.
I am whole
And blessed
As I take comfort
In your embrace.
I am aware, healed, and well.
Amen.

THE SECOND STEP OF THE HEALING PROCESS IS TO PROCLAIM OUR stories. To proclaim is to rise up and announce who we are with boldness and clarity. After seeing glimmers of who we are, through reclaiming ourselves, it's important to proclaim that story to others. But this step can be misunderstood. Here we do not look at "proclaiming" as the trumpet call of ego. Contemplating the content of the messages we put into the world is as significant as being aware of the messages we receive and internalize.

These dual messages are intrinsically connected. My aim is to encourage you to consciously co-create and seek out a community where your authenticity is cultivated and your journey furthered. Learn the difference between the messages your ego issues out of fear and the messages your soul wishes to share. This demands the challenge of knowing who you are and determining how you choose to authentically meet the world. It's like Ray Charles said: "I never wanted to be famous. I just wanted to be great." This is how you become the best version of yourself.

Why proclaim? Because with all the noise in our world, much of what is said is counterproductive to our journey. We all need to take more responsibility in combating counterproductive messages with our own authenticity! Humans thrive on stories. We construct much of our reality based on narratives we've processed and internalized. This makes us different from other life-forms, who simply react to stimuli. The society we live in today thrives on commercially pitching a marketed reality to you—a false reality that derails us and bends our journey to others' purposes. Sadly, it deepens the divide between us and our Stranger and distances us from harmony and unity.

A culture of greed is at its most profitable and productive when it is filling us with constant anxiety, dread, and insecurity. The job of the profit-making engine is to first sell the idea that "you" are some problem that needs to be solved, like an island in constant danger of invasion, and then to sell you placebos for the artificial conflicts it created. Dread narrative is the biggest industry of our era. We spend our lives hiding from imagined fears and creating terrorists to fight when we should really start by turning off the terror on our televisions and inviting a neighbor over for coffee. We cannot hope to rise above the corrupt paradigm meekly or in silence. First we must reclaim our own story, and then we must proclaim it, and make noise, too! In presenting an alternative to that anxious narrative through telling our authentic stories, we share who we are and can connect others to their own authenticity as they continue to help refocus us as well, growing our strength.

Someone called the other day wanting to know about my work, and in the middle of the conversation she said how refreshing it was to speak with a man who is direct and seems to be in touch with himself. How empowering! But when did that happen? During my last few days, when walking, I allowed feelings to arise, and I returned to the following questions: Who am I? Where have I been? We are inclined to plumb the deepest depths to answer questions like that, but a plethora of answers might appear right on the surface when we examine even our most basic needs and actions.

On one visit back from college, feeling unfocused, I asked my father if I could take a few minutes to breathe and quiet myself before joining the family in the living room. His retort was that I could breathe in the living room. Realizing that no quiet moment was imminent, I entered with frazzled energy. I carried that energy with me. *Boundaries* didn't exist in the family lexicon, but *pleasing* and *pretending* played a large part. Expectations and unspoken assumptions were the cornerstone of our family foundation, as became evident whenever I did something that broke the unspoken rules.

Even before memory, I, like so many of us, was conditioned to betray my most basic needs. As children, we proclaim so loudly! But as adults we are silent unless we are drunk. What delusion! After a while, we lose touch of the compass inside, the one that can guide us to health, and we fail to hear our own message.

Our days are punctuated by almost constant communication. The problem isn't that we don't make noise, it is that so often we're echoing our culture, and what we're telling each other is crap. We meander off the track and make small talk, in turn making ourselves small. The world doesn't need more bullshit about the weather, more catcalls, holy rollers, and fish tales. Our world needs empowered, contemplative, intimate strangers with their eyes wide open, acting as beacons for ourselves and others on the path to healing.

Too often, we settle for becoming commercials for ourselves, and then *we* become placebos for the health and fullness we are really seeking. Yet we continue to suffer, feeling endlessly unfilled. We make ourselves sick with our excuses: Oh, I've been living my mom's story. Oh, I'm a footnote of my culture. Oh, I've accepted a marginalized view of myself that profited the cruel person who sold it to me. Oh, this is what my peer group has told me I should be in order to make them feel more comfortable.

Stop living a life where your meaning is defined by cultivating and selling the illusion of your stability and success to strangers. Instead, focus on actually accomplishing those things for yourself in a meaningful way! Your story will be much more interesting, I promise. And you'll sleep better.

Then make some noise! Once we get in touch with our own stories, we learn to filter truth from deception. We learn to face reality rather than fear it. We've been living these illusionary stories to fit in and find self-worth, when in fact self-worth is attainable only through knowing and sharing who we truly are. To do this, we can't tiptoe through our lives; we have to walk in all the way. Only then can we share the truth of who we really are. Only then do we have a foundation to build upon.

As we get in touch with our truth, we confront things we may have hidden for so many years—everything from being the good boy to not talking back in school to fears of failure—we uncork the bottle and become more able to express what we want and what matters to us. Proclaiming is a process that allows what is welling up within us to arise to the surface and break free. In a time that condones passive-aggressive behavior, where living in fear of individuality is the norm, speaking your essence is a genuine way of being.

By doing this within your community, rather than in isolation, you announce that it is not a narcissistic exercise but the act of an equal, carving out space for yourself among equals. You have a voice to combat the endless media blitz, advertisements, billboards, and phobias that play at deafening volume in our modern times.

Let me explain how I've experienced the difference proclaiming made in my own life. Proclaiming can take many forms. For example, in the midst of my trials with Hodgkin's lymphoma, I learned that succumbing to voices louder than my own was detrimental to my health because they overrode my own instincts. Once I understood my truth, I had to proclaim it and advocate for myself in order to get the care I needed and heal fully.

One evening the senior oncologist came into my tiny, windowless hospital room to tell me he thought the cancer had advanced to my lungs, and he wanted to schedule another surgery. The hospital sent in the social worker to console me and offer guidance. She suggested that I refrain from buying the house I'd planned to purchase for my family. Of course, I was despondent at the idea of surgery as well as the discouragement of my plans, and furthermore, what I felt inside myself—what I experienced in my own meditations—was that my lungs looked pink and healthy.

Still, the surgery was to proceed.

Then, after the counselor attempted to navigate my life choices for me, the night before the procedure, the resident surgeon sat beside me on the bed. "Look, we know the cancer is in your lungs," he said. "This surgery is just a formality."

I was incensed by what I perceived as an unexamined declaration of my inner workings. I was also struck by the lack of openness in the decision-making process. Furious, I hopped out of bed to let the nurses know if this man was supposed to be involved with my surgery, it would need to be postponed. I am not negating the function or value of doctors, or teachers, or scientists, or holy men, or general authorities in our lives. But when someone tries to supplant "you" with their concept of you or your situation and beliefs, it is time to get a second opinion. And that opinion needs to come from YOU.

Much of the confusion we humans experience is over whether we should or shouldn't speak about who we are, whether we should proclaim it clearly and loudly, or stuff it down deeper. Should I speak up for myself in this hospital room, or should I simply be quiet and defer to the "expert," ignoring the truth of myself as equal? Especially when we are scared or vulnerable, it can seem easier to stay silent or to just bow to prevailing practice. Again, we are seeking that illusion of safety. We say: "I'm just a part of this institution, this gender, this church, this country, this family," and turn on the autopilot. But why, then, are we blessed with that nagging inner voice that demands more? I don't serve anyone by being on autopilot; I serve by showing up fully prepared to be an active participant in my own life. I serve by proclaiming.

Proclaiming has little to do with ego and much to do with empowering the self. Seeing your true self is the extraordinary mystical understanding that you have your own identity and at the same time are a part of something larger. We each have a light, which is part of a larger light.

During college, as I struggled to differentiate myself from the person my father and rabbi wanted me to be, I learned to cultivate my light, and self, in the quiet company of the Quakers. George Fox, founder of the Religious Society of Friends, read the Jesus of the Christian Gospel of John as an eternal Christ, rather than a historical one. Quaker ethics are based on feeling over reason, and Quakers believe that the eternal Christ is within all of us, acting as a sort of compass to help us navigate. That means we're all equal and can listen to the sacred directly, without the need for clerical intermediaries. It's just a matter of quieting the mind, listening, and at times, sharing with the community.

Similarly, in the Jewish mystical story of the Zohar, we learn that the firmaments of light came down from God because one strong light was too much for humans to receive all at once. So, the light was divided up into an infinite number of sweet little lights, like pieces of a broken mirror, each holding the same vast, eternal image, and they all have to interrelate with one another to re-create the whole.

While speaking your truth, we must also learn to fully listen to others proclaim their truths without our judging, manipulating, or projecting. When we listen to and honor each sacred self, we live in truth. While I've said before that, in the broadest sense, safety is an illusion, there is still considerable merit in finding communion in an accepting and nurturing environment. People fear that overt honesty will alienate them. But in reality, when you accept this openness and demand it of others, you will find that you still connect with others—and in a deeper, more meaningful way.

At the same time, if you demand this honor of others, you have to be willing to show up and offer the same. In the mid-1980s in Sonoma County, I had one of my most profound experiences of proclaiming, listening to, and honoring stories. I was about three years out of seminary and had just returned to California after working at a Unitarian church in Virginia. I was wrestling with many questions: What is worship? What are we doing when we come together in that way? How do we channel the sacred? I wanted a community in which people of all backgrounds could come together to explore these questions together. There were still traditions, hierarchies, dogmas, and prescribed politics in the current religious culture that I found detrimental to my spiritual healing process. I decided that I wanted to take it further. I wanted everyone to be able to honor their sacred selves and live in truth.

I left the Quaker and Unitarian umbrellas and created Interspirit. I was influenced by my time in the seminary, which was, at that point, the most fulfilling juncture of my spiritual odyssey. Interspirit was a "post-religious" response to what I missed about going to school in Berkeley, when I was thrown into the middle of a smörgåsbord of people of all different faith groups, generally unified in the authenticity of their shared existential processes. That was an exciting time for me; the environment of sharing ideas, of reclaiming and proclaiming, exemplified the difference between the work of the Unitarian Transcendentalist pioneers, which created the organization, and the more rigid hierarchy that had come to helm it and into which I had unintentionally drifted.

I realized I'd been wandering deeper into the desert and decided it was time to branch out and create a new group with a clear intent. Still just shy of the age of online social networking, I poured my longing into planning this new idea I had, Interspirit. I began advertising for a "post-religious" meeting and discussion group, and I left flyers around town, hoping to reel in like-minded pilgrims.

About a dozen people responded, and our group was born. Step by step, it became so much more than I ever expected or intended. Originally, I rented a space for us to meet, but soon we were meeting in my home in Petaluma. At first we met once a week, but soon we were gathering more often.

Initially, I thought the group would grow, that we would regularly welcome new members, but we soon got into such intimate and profound truth-telling that we decided not to openly solicit others any longer.

At the time I had a large, open house, because I like to tear walls down, internally and quite literally. When Interspirit gathered, we would meet in the living room and move over to the dining room. In addition to sharing stories and ourselves, we always shared a meal and broke bread together, as home-based spiritual and religious communities have done for thousands of years. This cultivated ritual had a unique mandala effect: we created the meal; we consumed the meal; and the value was in our presence with one another.

Our members reflected the many ways divine light can shine in different humans. We were men and women; gay and straight; Muslim, Christian, Jewish, fundamentalist, and more. And we shared a goal: to come together with awareness, without doing harm to each other.

Our times together were our Sabbaths, a time set aside for worship in its highest form—a union with the Divine with no impediment or intermediary. How did we accomplish that? With depth and sensitivity. Our group was established with respect and honored each person. We stated at the first gathering that we were coming together intentionally to explore the roots of our individual journeys and to value both where we came from and where we were going.

Coming together with intention, through choice, was an idea some of us didn't initially understand. And although the unknowing felt uncomfortable at first, we found that our discomfort helped guide us. We realized that we were in control of our discomfort some of the time—but not all of the time. We proclaimed our truths despite our discomfort, and we came to a deeper understanding: we affirmed that all of us were whole, complete *beings*.

One of the most significant experiences we shared was crafting a spiritual autobiography, attempting to understand the circumstances of our lives in a spiritual context. Over the course of two months we explored different components of this context. For instance, one week, I posed the question, "Where was your safe place as a child?" I offered art supplies and invited everyone to draw this place and use the drawing as a starting point to share stories. I invite you to do the same. Imagine the idea of your own spiritual autobiography. Start with the first step. What would you call it?

One person struggled with this invitation to draw a safe space. She shared that she'd felt threatened for much of her childhood. For years, she didn't have a home to feel secure in.

When she was finished sharing, I felt the stunned witnesses in the room. I knew there was nothing else to say right then and wanted everyone to sit with what had been shared before anyone spoke in response. "That's it for tonight," I said. "Let's go home."

Up until this moment in Interspirit, this woman had never told anyone these things. It's hard to imagine all the false narratives and judgments she must have felt in that silence. In our group she finally found the environment she needed to share that story, proclaim her truth, and feel affirmed.

Each person's childhood story was so different, spanning limitless possible human configurations, yet they were all about the common human yearning to connect. Proclaiming is a way of connecting to the larger human story, which is a vital part of healing fully.

After that meeting of sharing drawings and stories, one by one, members allowed themselves explore more deeply with each other. It was as though we'd all been saving our stories for the right time and place of caring so that we were able to share. I made sure to join in the proclaiming, offering the story of being diagnosed with cancer and the often harrowing road I took toward healing. I shared how I found healing through being completely present and in knowing myself as a being not separate in my pain, but connected to and in relationship with all beings.

In Interspirit, the self-absorption with the superficial and with the artificial boundaries of our egos began to fade. People no longer apologized for their self-perceived limited drawing or writing skills. People began to see who they each really were: a unique gift given to humanity. Coming from the same source, however, each of us could perceive that in our own way. It was liberating! By proclaiming our stories in our own particular ways, we shared the gifts of ourselves with each other.

We also shared a Passover Seder, largely in the Jewish tradition. One of the couples was a beautiful example of individual paths coming together. One partner was Muslim, the other Jewish. The Muslim man wanted to invite his parents to our sacred gathering, so I had the unique opportunity of crafting a Seder that was universal enough to welcome and include his parents.

Sharing this Seder was deeply moving, so much so that I've done it every year since. In a typical Seder, the focus is on the outward story and history of the Jewish people rather than on considering the teachings for what they have to say about the inner lives of those present. But I structured our Seder as a journey of inner liberation, so that it would have meaning for everyone there, regardless of religious background. And every year, I make sure we eat well and have fun embracing the renewing energy of spring.

We can easily recognize ourselves as gifts when we resonate with our unique vibration. When those vibrations connect, we first find harmony, and then a symphony. Perhaps in your healing quest, you might find a little peace in perceiving unity and creation through that concept. If only my introductory physics class so many years ago related how each member of the class vibrated at a unique frequency, I might have understood physics. Many years later, I'm aware of how each of us uniquely experiences and perceives self and the world and responds accordingly. I can just sit next to someone and literally feel their beat, at times in sync with my own, and at other moments discordant, out of sync. Now I'm more aware of the nature of attraction, and I listen to my inner guide before making choices. How do you find the balance to make social decisions? Take a minute and evaluate.

My unique vibration feels to me like a jazz piece sung by a female voice, moving from slow and quiet—almost inwardly directed—to bebop, climbing the scales and back again, meditating and dancing seamlessly.

When blended together with respect and honor, our individual vibrations produce the symphony of life. By taking the risk of sharing our stories, we acknowledge, honor, and affirm each other. Together we form the integrity of a "we."

During our time together in Interspirit, members of the group were making life-changing decisions, and as our meetings continued, people felt that the group played a pivotal role in their lives. We became more empowered to see ourselves as divine sparks, forming a sacred light together. In this group we discovered that sharing our stories and proclaiming ourselves was a reverent act. Learning to witness the ordinary as holy created a space of stillness and contentment.

Later, as my journey and geographical hopscotch continued, I remained inspired by Interspirit. I started other workshops in Oregon, New Zealand, and elsewhere. To me, this journey was largely about planting seeds. Each time, I listened deeply and, as I learned, massaged the content and structure. Each experience was profound and unique as a group of humans came together to bring ourselves out in the air, to proclaim our stories and to gain support and sustenance for doing the work of living in truth.

My experiences with Interspirit confirmed how enriching it is for people to touch and be touched. It is a true gift when we share our stories with people who care and listen and, in turn, share their stories with us. When we announce ourselves with boldness and clarity, the world seems like much less of an enemy. We find that we attract what we need at this place in our journey. As we connect with each other and weave our stories together, our lives become a rich tapestry, and we come to know our connection as a sacred covenant, which we will further investigate in the next chapter.

PRACTICE

Here are some questions for you to consider, to start you on your path to proclaiming. How do you know when what you feel as a trigger is an invitation toward a deeper inner truth? Think of some times in your life when you were dared to grow beyond your comfort zone. The sense of danger and risk can feel almost like a craving. What did you feel, and how did you respond to the call?

What does the Sabbath mean to you, and how would you encounter it? How do you feel your chosen community impacts your journey? What do you share with the world about yourself and your truth? What would you *like* to share?

Now I want you to take a few minutes to practice and proclaim. Consider this idea of a spiritual autobiography—not a Hollywood blockbuster, or a Bible, or a soap opera, or a sports game. No one's narrative but your own; your own spiritual autobiography. What would the first line say? Find a place, now, peacefully, eagerly, not in any rush...and write it out. See where the exercise leads you.

On the next few pages, you will find more of my poetry, which I share to proclaim my truth, in the spirit of communion and unity.

WHAT IS MY NAME

What is my name,
And who am I?
A village in Russia
Where poverty and family pride
Intermingled in a community
Of shared pain
So great it can't be spoken.
A name when it arrived
Was given by the guard,
And different for each brother,
So terrible it can't be spoken
To the sons and daughters;
Only look forward
With faith—
A little more fragile,
Splintered in many villages
Along the journey.
The hope that we can stay
Coming in and out at will
That we may choose
To be with all the rest.
But what is my name,
And who am I
As I marry the white princess
And spread my seed,
Offering to the world new birth
Who knew they are just Divine?
A part of the whole,
No longer the tribal village—
A child of all.
But what is their name,
And who are they?

THE BOARDWALK

The boardwalk called
To the members of all families
In the community of memory,
With its intoxicating smells
Of sea air and saltwater
And its seductive smile
That beckoned one and all
To its promise of wonder
And fantasy.

All winter, the rows
Of garage doors
Stood hibernating for hundreds of blocks,
Gathering strength for the long
Days and nights of summer
When the quiet and desolation
Of winter's long cold nights
Gave way to a calliope
Of games, rides, and food—
Enough to make safe
For families to surrender
To its embrace.
Gramma sitting with all the other
Bubbies, playing pokeno;
Dad engaged in poker,
Or any game
That made room
For philosophy and current events;
And the moms
Sipping coffee or Italian ice,
For in those moments
There was no need to control
The First Born
Who were in the waves, or
Under the boardwalk,
Exploring anatomy and chemistry

Without the guilt or fear
Of a life half-lived.

So summer brought moments
Of grace
To an otherwise scripted childhood
Where the First Born would succeed
And make his mom proud.

THE FOOL

Your father is a fool,
As I carried you on my back
Listening to Thoreau
Recite his words
Of harmony and individuation,
Bringing you to the
Schoolhouse so the
Students could learn
Of the child of love.

Watching you go off
To school as I cried
The tears of joy,
Supporting your
Right to learn
So your soul
Would soar:
Such a fool as I
Only knows the trials
Of learning life
While trying to
Give to the other.
Hard and fragile as
Life can be,
We make decisions
With grace, I hope—
But not always,
For we don't know all.

I could not just watch.
Fathers are actors,
Not audience,
All the time.
And so in the scheme
Of things
With love and pain,

We take the risks
Expecting life to win,
Hoping love to last
And friendship to grow.

I AM A MAN

I am a man
Who held a baby
As her head emerged
With her crown proudly
Announcing her right
To be here.

I am a man
Who reinforced
A woman's back
As she pushed hard
So in her breaths
The crown could appear.
And I am a man
Who entered the battlefields
Of commerce
With armor enclosing my heart
Till it couldn't cry anymore.

But—I am also the man
Who welcomed the
Tears of love
In moments of grace,
Crying at the schoolhouse
Watching children
Being allowed to be,
Or seeing you smile
So far it shattered my shell
Of veneer.

And I am the man
Who met death on the pathway,
Signaling for a later time, as
There are people waiting
For me to hold them
And take care.

I want a new story
To open my heart
So I can cry in
The playground with all the children
And prosper together
Because we learned
How to share.

I want another beginning
That says it's okay to ask
For help and still be strong;
An opening that knows
In union we are whole,
Meeting each other
As though we have always
Known love, even in the sorrow.

I am a man who wants to enter
Your doorway and walk into your soul
Fully naked,
Melting into your embrace.

CHAPTER THREE

Opening

Yesterday I was clever; I wanted to change the world.
Today I am wise; I am changing myself.

RUMI

COVENANT

I am blessed to have
The privilege and a life
That asks me to commit to my word;
For now, I can offer
Myself fully or just partially to you.
Who is there to blame
For living my choice?
And so I ask for guidance
To remember
Who I am.
Amen.

Ask not what the universe can do for you; ask what you can do for the universe!

Beyond the insights of self-clarity and the stripping away of social consumer preprogramming lies a deeper hunger. I feel it. You feel it. We have discussed how to love and respect our identities. We will evaluate the choices and commitments we require to honor our truest self and intention. To do this is to open. In opening, we access those dormant seeds within us and learn to bloom.

What we need most is to learn to honor our deep, profound, spiritual connection. Now we will focus on identifying the root of that connection so that we may open ourselves to it. We will do this by witnessing the connective spark that links us to the Divine within and learning to recognize that same divinity within our neighbor. We will look at the light we share in both the finite and infinite realms, and we will seek to communicate with it authentically.

We have taken initial steps together. We've looked at reclaiming our sense of identity from our culture. And we have looked at proclaiming that identity and emboldening ourselves through community. Moving forward with our next step, I am asking you to continue to redefine your notion of self.

I am asking you to open further and dig deeper inwardly while connecting more broadly outwardly. This might sound both redundant and contradictory. But bear with me; it is not. Both of those first steps were crucial in bringing you closer to being able to open. Now we will enact that opening on multiple levels.

Of all the deceptions foisted upon us by society, perhaps the most perilous is what I call the grand disconnection. *You are your Facebook page. You are brand-name shoes. You are judged by the size of your*

television or by your perfect green lawn or by your witty bumper sticker.
All these underlying messages lead you to believe that you are an
island, defined by your potential as a consumer. I have news for you.
You are *NOT* an island. You are the universe.

One of my greatest inspirations in discovering the truth is spiritual wisdom master and author Martin Buber, who emphasized that
"life is all about meeting. Meeting is the coming together where an 'I'
communes with a 'Thou' and, in so doing, meets. And meeting asks
that we commit to our word and deed with integrity and care." Thus,
we must learn to open beyond ourselves, to bloom, to invite dormant divinity to reawaken and articulate its mystery and direction
within us.

As I have said, within each of us is a spark, a light, which leads
back to a bigger light. I want to expound on the full implications of
this idea. When we contemplate divinity, and when we address our
neighbor, we hit that same wall of disconnection from ourselves. You
are a ship piloted by your identity in many ways. You *are* unique and
beautiful. These are truths we do not need to sacrifice. But at the same
time, we cannot allow this truth to distract us from a deeper truth:
All is One. Within all creation is a spark of the Creator, placed inside
of us to translate the infinite to us in the context of this reality and
to guide us to our truest self, which I think of as home, our center.

You are you. By now I hope you are learning to rejoice in that!
Within you is also the deep seed of divinity. Within your neighbor,
your lover, your parent, and your child, the same seed exists. This
seed, this light, however you perceive it, was placed there to tether
us both to the spirit of our creation and to one another. By opening
into this, we evolve. So, while we are all very different, there is a real
unity within that connects us all. The problem is that many of us
have trained ourselves to no longer perceive this seed, and we have
not taken the time to help it grow. It is a profitable trick of society to
disconnect you from that reality of deep connection. An island is easier to conquer than a universe. A lonely soul feels lost. Disconnection
helps the material world lay claim on your soul. These are lies that
have been whispered to you your whole life and then gift-wrapped.

Now that you have opened yourself to experiencing a deeper reality, it is time to pursue divinity.

The trick here is to retrain yourself. Learn to witness divinity within you and learn to seek it out in others. Open to the idea of a much vaster sense of self. The greatest tyranny is that which robs you of your truest self. Don't help those who profit by doing so! We live in a world where the institutions of spirituality have been systematically robbed of their virtue by the ambition of humankind. We are conditioned to hide from words once sacred, like *covenant* or *communion*, because their meanings have been diluted in order to confuse and control us. But no dogma can lay claim to the truth these words imply, nor to the truths inside of us. The time to fear the meanings of words created to connect you to a deeper peace has passed. In opening to them, you can commune with the Divine.

Let me share an experience I had with my own opening to help clarify this process. Many times in my adult life, I have felt small while pursuing something I thought would fulfill me. Have you ever felt that way? I felt small in my second marriage, and as such, I was unable to show up fully. I was unable to proclaim my truth and be heard. I'd made a sacred promise from my heart to my wife, believing it was understood and valued. My ego said "maintain," while my heart said "stop." Eventually, after four years abroad, we returned to the States and divorced soon after.

This period, post-divorce, became the most painful time of my life. But the broken covenant and destruction of the relationship wasn't what caused the most pain. The pain came from a deeper place, and all my other broken relationships resurfaced to haunt me and reinforce the ache.

If we could connect the rungs of our emotional choices, we could see that we ascend and descend continually. There is no straight line to follow out of the pain. Usually the patterns in our lives are more like circles or spirals. There is, however, the opportunity to open to deeper truths about yourself.

I realized I was still responding to the same old unresolved issues. So, I returned to working on myself, and this work took me far back.

Through deep guided meditation, I realized the relationship that needed my most devoted attention and healing was within myself. I needed to understand my purpose. In meditation, I sat with my seven-year-old self, and he sat with me, compassionate witnesses to each other's pain.

What is the significance of this communion and connection with one's younger self? I had to learn to reopen to such deep wisdom within myself. The world and reality itself are much different to a seven-year-old. We forget the secrets we knew in our youth. We forget the promises we have made within ourselves to this world regarding the people we vowed to one day become.

The biggest shift is our ability to love and our need to connect with one another. We replace those needs with what you might call "survival instinct" or an acceptance of "how the world works." But this line of thinking is bullshit. The world we make for ourselves is the world we occupy. The question is: What is the world we make compared to the world that has been made for us?

This juncture is where the significance of communion enters, and where I must further define what I mean by opening. We can't have a relationship with the sacred, with the Divine, while in an "I" frame of mind. It has to be that you are *being with* and therefore *being in* a place of quiet, where you are paying attention to, listening to, and engaging with the other. You need to open to create that shared space and see the unity and singularity of this shared connection.

Simply put, you must learn to see God in yourself and see it in every other soul you encounter. Boy, that would make for a different world, wouldn't it? For me, the word *open* takes on all of that significance. It's a word that many humans struggle with today, because we like to pay attention to our own ego and persona rather than be in that open place of truly connecting with one another.

Many of us have an idea of a spirituality that is largely rhetorical. We dialogue with or direct our thinking toward some form of textbook God. Instead of getting involved within the community, we have a one-way relationship with a Higher Power. We pray for things we want, make promises we rarely keep, and see God as a form of superstitious luck that owes us something for our trouble.

This is an abstract and inauthentic approach to faith. Like many of the solutions we are duped into wanting, it, too, is microwaved, the spiritual equivalent of fast food. Many of us learned to worship this way when we were young—the same way we learned about Santa Claus. We learned from a culture that didn't demand more and used religion as a system of control. We need to go back to that wilderness within and reevaluate this idea of a fundamental separation. Have you gained from it, or has it left you feeling like something is missing? Do you see life as the beautiful gift it is? Or is it a game to play, or worse, something to merely endure?

Let's work on opening your soul's purpose. We find the strangest obstacles. During my second marriage and afterward, I came to a crisis of purpose. I felt so profoundly in love that I lost myself. Without considering myself during the relationship or the importance of a reciprocal covenant in marriage, I moved from Oregon to New Zealand to Tasmania, sharing in a story not fully realized and not my own.

Marriage is a noble institution. Many of our pursuits and distractions have noble intentions. Thich Nhat Hanh has spoken at length about the Vietnam War; he watched so many of his fellow monks go to great lengths to explore the nature of peace and violence. He also deeply studied the American opposition to the war. In writing about the American peace community and how we could make meaningful stands and statements, he asked how we could march, argue, fight, and do all kinds of wonderful things, only in order to create dissension? The pacifist agenda is noble, but endeavoring to make it happen it with malice, drugs, false euphoria, and avarice is not a suitable path toward an ascending ideology. He knew, in our reactionary zeal, that we had forgotten something. Hanh asked the question, "Do we know how to love? And do we know how to love in the midst of real-life pain?"

The same can be said for a bad marriage. The answer is trying to speak to us, from that divinity inside. When I was seven, I loved. I loved deeply. I had not yet learned an alternative way of being.

Humanity was my family. This was my most authentic form as a spiritual being. But how easily life can blow us off course! The man-made world is eager to offer us placebos. To right myself and return to my path, I had to make (and continually reevaluate) my openness to and covenant of love with the divinity within me, in order to end the little wars I waged that kept me from my truest path.

This process isn't easy. Your ego will bleed. And the world will double down in its efforts to force conflict upon you. Society is cultivating you to be afraid. It's scary to come off your island! That's why you must open to the universe. I think about all of these events—global and personal—in the context of the word *healing*. Healing is really about making whole, bringing together. Healing doesn't only take place in a singular body, and it's not something that can be given or presented to you. We heal through our communion with creation and through our recommitment to the unique path each of us is intended for.

We heal when we no longer see separation between ourselves and our neighbors. Their pain is our pain, and our pain is theirs. The same is true for joy. All emotion is creation expressing itself, and with the strength of that creation, we can flourish beyond our individual suffering. The Buddhists say that life is suffering; this process of opening is the tool we need to wake up and accept a reality larger than our individualized perceptions. Healing and growth bind the universe—not division and separateness. The way to heal ourselves and our planet is to acknowledge the communion we share and to honor our covenant's honest intent.

Why are we here? That's the big question. Let me suggest that some answers are too big to be learned alone. And so, we share this reality to gain wisdom. As W. Somerset Maugham famously noted, "It is easy to be a holy man on top of a mountain." But away from the mountain, picking our way among the minefields of our everyday lives, we learn the practical significance of the lessons of the universe. To do this we must open—to ourselves, to one another, and to divinity.

Perhaps a more immediate question is not why we exist, but rather, why we exist here together. Let me share a story with you from my own experience that may help clarify why merely coexisting is not the full exploration of our entwined fates.

When I worked at the community college in West Virginia, I lived a mile down a dirt road that was mostly clay. In this "holler," which is like a small valley, four neighbors lived: Lem and Bobbie, Chuck, and me.

I was a twenty-something urban radical, while Lem and Bobbie were politically and religiously conservative, salt-of-the-earth folks. We obviously had disagreements about our differing approaches to life. But every year during the rainy season, when the clay became mud so deep that the road would almost disappear and even a truck with four-wheel drive would get stuck in it, we would go out together—without question and without disagreement—and put in new culverts and grade the road and do whatever was needed so that we, and others, could come and go freely. And it became our tradition to share a meal together after our many hours of work.

There was also an unspoken agreement that whoever lived on the road would help and then share the meal; we were a community. What we agreed or disagreed on; whether we voted Democrat or Republican; whether we believed in Jesus, Buddha, or any one of a million other options—none of that was as important as working together as a community so that all of us could get to our homes and back out again to do our daily chores.

For us neighbors along that dirt road, the moments of mutual engagement were far more profound than our occasional debates and arguments, all of which dissipated rather quickly. Our unspoken covenant together was bigger than our individual pettiness or self-righteousness.

For all of us, the purpose of our lives and of the function we share transcends our individual egos. The lessons of the world will always be bigger than the minds comprehending them. The best we can do is analyze our pieces of wisdom and the wisdom offered us by others as gifts of equal value. There is no value, in this scenario, in remaining an island. We must open to one another.

We need this kind of connection in order to survive, and also to thrive. We are lured into technologies that falsely promise to facilitate communication, and it is easy to forget the basic truth life offers: we still need one another, in real time; breathing the same air, allowing interactions with each other and with the world, experiencing time and space together, being in each other's presence. The connection we share is not symbolic; it is tangible and it reveals its purpose constantly when we open.

One understanding of opening may be as a way to get "home." We'll discuss home more later, but for now, I mean home as the home of the heart. When we operate out of balance and in extremes—my way or your way—we miss the gifts of the more authentic, unique path we have been set upon. This process of connecting is the journey we require to finally come home to our true selves and to each other.

Once you see the importance of connecting to one another's needs and see your symbiosis with the well-being of others, you will see how it affects so many different aspects of your life. For instance, that unspoken agreement between parent and child is a covenant that endures no matter how old the child may be.

I revisited this truth powerfully when I was diagnosed with Hodgkin's disease. In my family, there may be such a thing as too much *being with*. Because of this extreme sense of closeness, my family was often deeply emotional regarding the health and welfare of other family members, but that concern also extended to petty things. When I was growing up, if a glass fell off the table, it was like a world war. How could this have happened, and would we all survive? In my family, we were always in each other's business, and often upset about it. I never knew when the next ever-looming storm was going to break, and I didn't know there were such things as boundaries.

So, many years later, when I learned I had Hodgkin's, it became important for me to figure out how to communicate with my parents in a way that would soften their fears, which I knew would be swift and immediate, and also avoid causing myself additional stress. I wanted to create an environment that allowed for nurturing and support of what I was going through. So, rather than saying, "Hey! I've got Hodgkin's disease!" I found it more beneficial to remind myself that there is a covenantal relationship between us and see it as an opportunity to discover how to communicate in a way that had the potential to bring us together.

Connection wouldn't come from calling up my parents on the phone and bluntly delivering the news. Instead, I translated myself through words in a different way and sent them a letter. Of course, once they received the letter, they called and still went bonkers. But the letter did help. It created space for me as I gave them the information. My phone conversation with them still left me shaking, but it felt contained. In the midst of their emotional breakdown, I had managed to create one tiny pocket of containment I could crawl into while still being an honest, loving son and claiming my own need as well. I found a way to commune with myself and with them in a way that was conducive to healing.

I like the difference between "In *the* beginning" and "In *a* beginning." In *a* beginning, I am continually open to surprise, knowing I'm not in control. When we're always open to new beginnings, to the possibility of softening, of not knowing and being surprised, we find more truths and solutions that previously lay hidden beyond our limited perception.

Here's another story from my own life. I like to take long walks, and I particularly enjoy getting lost in new places throughout the world. One time I got lost was when I was looking for a house in Hobart, Tasmania, for our family. I happened upon a woman gardening in her front yard, and we got to chatting. She invited me in for tea and she and her family became dear friends. We even lived with them for a couple of months!

It is better to create doors and windows than walls within ourselves. However, I know it is difficult to think about opening and connecting when our minds are scattered and have lost their discipline. Pain is a huge factor in this development. My mind has been open to ideas, thoughts, emotions, and friends for many years now. I think of myself as an empty vessel eagerly accepting and waiting for input. But I know these qualities were for a long time the by-products of blindly pursuing hungers and cravings when I was lost.

So, my journey has taken many turns, and I was without a map or guide in many cases, as are you. But working without a map doesn't mean working without a compass. When I made choices without being open to my inner divinity, I found myself spiritually floundering. Sometimes, forgoing the illusion of safety in favor of our heart's true direction is our true empowerment. When I made choices by communing with myself and the universe, I felt stronger and happier.

Opening to your communion with the Divine demands concentration and reflection; you must give yourself the gift of "dynamic rest," by which I mean a kind of continuous, quiet, evolving dialogue with your Stranger. Restoring your covenant to yourself comes from knowing yourself and what you want. It also comes from knowing what you have to offer others. If your wants are shallow and self-serving, and if what you have to offer comes from a place of disconnection and self-containment, what do you expect to receive from the universe?

When approaching your inner divinity, consider the qualities of Shabbat, the separating of ordinary time into a liminal (threshold) time for contemplating the Divine—this is where you can find what I call dynamic rest. We are creatures of habit, and the exciting thing is that we can reprogram ourselves to create healthy, life-renewing habits. We can remember our story, our true nature, by saying yes to the gift that is us.

When things were bad, I remember my wise friend Warren said one day, "Arnie, your pericardium is too permeable." I was in damage control mode, trying to patch the holes and bring in reinforcements, until I realized I wasn't living my life, I was merely existing. And floundering. We all hurt in this life. Some people still manage to float to the top and be their best selves. How can you take that pain, that grief, and that weight and come back to "Yes"? I had to open and become more than myself by surrendering to a deeper connection. I had to think in a language of love. I had to choose love, as part of my invitation, and you can, too.

Deciding to be open spiritually is another pivotal moment when you are pursuing a path of healing—and you will know it when the shift occurs. The emotions we evaluate our life with are valuable, but they are neither objective nor permanent. So, when we offer ourselves to the Creator, should we not come from a place of connection—of "Yes"—rather than from emotion and "Maybe," "I'm not good enough," or "I don't have enough time"?

If we turn our appeal toward a Creator, we must recall that we are not the sole creation and that the chasms between our interests and the interests of others are manufactured not by God but by us. We must learn to master this deeper opening.

Opening to spaciousness can be overwhelming at times. It is important to have sangha ("beloved community," a Buddhist term), teachers, guides, and friends who can guide and offer support. We have the ongoing capacity to grow, and we are always evolving. G. I. Gurdjieff talks about our being machines with the capacity of being human through "work." The Buddha, too, taught that we have the capacity to evolve through practice, or the "work" of living rightly. Opening gives us hope to evolve, move forward, and never remain stuck in or defined by our limitations. Sometimes, our openness to others can inspire our own evolution, empower us with choices, and help us feel in control of our lives. Of course, by its nature, opening can take many directions.

One person who taught me so much about the magic openness was Chet. I met Chet in Santa Rosa, California, at the Quaker meeting. Most members of the meeting were in their seventies or eighties, with the exception of myself, my wife, Emily, and our daughters. Chet and his wife, Betty, soon became like godparents and grandparents to the girls. Most Sundays, after meetings, we went over to Chet and Betty's home for some lunch, conversation, and fellowship.

Even now, I can't speak or write about them without feeling both of their spirits fill me with waves of extraordinary joy. They were quiet, powerful people who smiled almost all the time. When I remember them, I feel God entering my being—always.

I knew intuitively that Chet was imbued with an extraordinary connection to the sacred. In WWII, he was a conscientious objector who spent his years in a work camp.

On those quiet Sundays, he would simply sit with me in the moment, completely present, and give me everything he had. I would ask him what it was like to be a conscientious objector during that war. In WWII, on the heels of the Great Depression, everybody felt they had to be engaged. Vietnam was different. Whereas I did two years of community service and had a hand in choosing my work, Chet wasn't allowed to do community service or anything of his choice. He served in work camps, hard-labor assignments where the perception was as follows: *You are a bad boy who didn't follow the rules, and now you must be punished.*

Yet I never felt anger from Chet in the way he expressed what those years were like for him. I never saw a shift in the man, although I looked for it. I was raised in a highly emotional, reactive environment in New York, and if we disliked or didn't understand something—or, more to the point, feared something—emotion, generally anger, was how we'd deal with it. That was how we framed our reality. Chet, however, was balanced—detached, yet totally present, and in love with whomever he was with in a given moment. And he was a healing force in my life during a particularly challenging time. He saved my life both literally and spiritually on many occasions by taking me to the hospital when I collapsed and by communing with me when my spirits were low.

One day, right after my first chemo treatment, I was with Chet and a few other friends. I wanted to take a walk in the woods and they came along to make sure I could weather it in my condition. Soon after we started our hike, I collapsed! I didn't regain consciousness for a couple of days, when I found myself hooked up to an IV. Apparently, when I had disappeared inside myself, Chet and the others threw me into their VW bus and drove me back to Stanford. The doctors, who had followed a computer prescription, accidentally gave me too much chemo. If not for these men, I know I'd be dead.

After my first wife left, and I was living in Sonoma by myself, I gave all my stuff away to a senior center and made a pilgrimage to Ashland,

Oregon. In the meantime, Chet developed dementia that progressed in severity to Alzheimer's. He and Betty moved into a Quaker retirement community called Friends House, and soon after, he died.

I returned to California to celebrate the life of a man who'd given me the gift of friendship for ten years. The Quaker understanding is that we all have light within, and as such, we are sacred. We have the ongoing capacity to grow; we are always evolving. Similarly, Siddhartha, the first Buddha, realized that we are not stuck in a karmic cycle; rather, we have the capacity to evolve through the practice of our lives.

Quaker memorials are reflections on this journey and are executed in the same simple fashion as meetings for worship, wedding, or business and in the same unpretentious, powerful form: come in, be quiet, pay attention. I knew Chet lived this Quaker practice of "sit, pay attention, listen" through all of our conversations. At Chet's memorial, I began to know, on a much larger scale, who this man was and how his *being with* had touched many other lives as well.

Young people told stories of how Chet had helped them financially and academically. Elders talked about what it was like in the work camp with Chet, and how he was a light for people there. Many folks talked about patents that I didn't even know Chet had for concrete sewer pipes, and I learned that his real passion in his work was creating sanitation systems for water.

During the memorial at Friends House, where they had room for fifty people, hundreds came and filled the entire building, overflowing outside. What moved me wasn't the number of people who attended, but the great collective silence that was imbued with God, and then lifted in sacred, harmonious voice as the celebrants, one after the other, spoke. The proceedings were filled with a divine unity that inspired me. This was a man who had made peace in his lifetime.

I felt in awe of this man, my friend. I realized the divinity with him, and its impact in speaking to the divinity within me. In the work camps, he had been a riveter. Later he became an engineer. He infused the work he did for our country with the sense of *This is what we do if we are all God, and we do it quietly and without fanfare.* This was the man who broke bread with me most Sundays, smiling and sharing stories, some from his past, but mostly being present in the moment. This was the man who taught me so much about *being with*, about true communion.

———

I was always restless. Back in Ashland, Oregon, I'd followed my spiritual longings to return to a Jewish-inspired community called a *havurah*. I enjoyed many things about this Jewish renewal and my reconnection with myself as a Jew. I was reminded that the Tree of Life also has roots that need to be honored. But I also again found that overly strict adherence to precepts didn't make room for me to show up fully and connect with others. It didn't help me open.

About five years after Chet's death, on Rosh Hashanah, the Jewish New Year, I was listening to the chanting, reading yet again the words that were not my own, and I thought of Chet. I quietly put the book down. His divinity was speaking to mine again. I took a hike for the rest of the day, renewing my knowledge that I don't need someone else's scripture to guide my own listening. Though it is important to have teachers, guides, and mentors who can guide and offer support, especially through their examples, at the same time, our own choices and discernments are critical in order to bring in appropriate gifts.

Again I was drawn back to the quiet, to the place where we all hunger and long for connection and covenant, and I found it. Chet knew where that place was. I remembered a place I knew when I was seven, and when I returned there in a liminal place of reflection and openness, I reconnected with the world I knew then: vast, blooming, and connected by love. I remembered the promises I made to God and my own quest to fulfill them. I returned renewed, having bloomed openly within myself.

Another way I opened to the universe was by writing poetry. In the writing process, I was able to open wide and make space for the ultimate connection to appear. The words were flowing through me, tethering me to the divinity within, and I was making a circuit by translating that to the world. The call to craft poetry was yet another invitation into a portal where time is liminal and opening spreads through the universe.

I initially resisted the discomfort of letting inspiration in, of the intimacy of the muse, but eventually, after being awakened in the middle of the night once too often, I chose to listen. I chose to go in, cross the bridge, and communicate with inner knowledge and perception. In that space, the voice of my Stranger was waiting for me.

Now my doors are open wide all the time, and I can enter that dynamic, restful space at will. My connection to my Stranger guides and informs a more intuitive sense of knowledge beyond my mind. I can listen through my heart, which communicates with my mind, sending impulses throughout my body that eventually radiate outward, softening others. Coming from heart has opened more sensitive and caring ways of hearing and acting. This communion is a gift, which has expanded to how I see my life. Now I see no separation, no closure—only opening, blooming, regenerating.

Opening is indeed an important step in the overall healing process. Love and openness are the greatest offerings of life because they allow us to make a commitment to connection and hope. After we reclaim our stories, learn who we truly are, and proclaim that knowledge clearly, we are able to open more deeply and commune with the universe and God, as an equal partner in our own destiny. Once we learn that the Divine is a real and meaningful part of ourselves and our neighbors, our mentalities shift, and we become more spiritually present, always open to the magic in the lives we share.

As you move forward, now that you have learned to recognize and honor that voice within, I will help you find better ways to listen and identify the answers you seek and receive, using tools you have been practicing.

PRACTICE

As we reconnect to love, other gifts are revealed, including the gift of wonder. What truths have you lost along the way? What faith do you carry and how does it carry you?

Begin a practice of reencountering the world through the eyes of yourself as a child. What has shifted or changed? Try to act out of this place of listening by discerning the differences between that inner wisdom and the chatter of the masses. How does it feel to begin to trust your own inner guidance?

Learn to discern, and be willing to stumble along the way. Again, I encourage you to free-write to answer these questions for yourself. You may use my poetry over the next few pages as a source of inspiration.

IS WONDER A PART OF YOU?

Do you open
For the other,
Connection
Making sacred
Your time on earth?

Can you say yes,
Meeting fully,
As though God
Asked to come on home?

Is wonder
A part of you?
Do you long
For the sweet
Smell of juices
Awakening you
From slumber
With a kiss
Upon your lips?

Are you tingling
All over,
As though children
Are playing
With no inhibitions
Throughout your body?

Are you laughing yet?
So silly,
You know you're alive;
Then you are ready
To touch another.
You are now
Prepared to share

The gift of new birth;
Just be you.
Just be.
Be
God.

OH, GRIEF

Oh grief—
So bold and deep;
So tied to the other,
Longing to be heard
And engaged in dialogue
About simpler days,
Where laughter and joy
Filled the air,
With children laughing and playing,
Where hugging and kissing
Were done for their own sake.
Where have they gone,
And why did you have to come
In their place?
For all the nights
Shared with you,
In the dark I go for you
And us.
It bellows in fear,
For no one can get in.
No one is here to touch
And to stay,
No matter what or who
Comes for the soul.
Stay close;
Hold tight,
Because there is calm
Behind the unresolved pain.
Hold tightly, for
I need you to guide me
Through the passageways
That twist through corners
I dared not go alone.
Hold on, for I need to be loved
And caressed.
I need strength,
And I need you to care.

THERE'S ONLY US

Is the suffering mine?
Or is it ours?
When I experience pain
Does anyone else
Feel with me,
Or do you
Feel your own set of things?
Or do you feel at all?

Why do I have to suffer
At all?
Is the choice to be human
Doomed to be alone,
Even in a crowd?
And why can't we feel
Together?
Or do we, and
We're just too afraid
To ask,
Or too proud
To know
There's only us
After all—
And sharing
Is the only way
Out or in.

I HOLD MY HEART

I hold my heart these days
With both my hands
Clasped to feel the pain.
I feel the suffering of the
Ten thousand ways.
We are God's children,
Born to be free of will,
Yet we continue the hurt,
For our wounds are too deep.
Our lyre's harp does sound
The lonely chords
Of peoples closing their souls,
As the heart can't forebear
The choices of self-destruction.

I hold my heart
With both hands now
As I listen to the human cry
Make its way into
All of our cores.
Some may close down
To protect their treasonous way,
But I have no choice but
To open my heart every day
A little more, for we are
Truly all there is.

CHAPTER FOUR

Listening

Prayer is translation. A man translates himself into a child asking for all there is in a language he has barely mastered.

LEONARD COHEN

HOPE

I awake each morning
Looking forward to a new life,
Even when yesterday left me cold and
Feeling alone.
And just when I thought a bottom
Had been reached,
I can choose to open wide
With the wonder of a newborn
Reaching for the touch
Of hope—and you are always there.
Amen.

As you emerge from dormancy, blinking at the light and awakening to a profound acknowledgment of the divinity within you, the most important next step in your endeavor is to listen. By listening I mean learning how to sift through the barrage of messages you receive to truly recognize what that inner voice is trying to say to you. We must develop practices that enable us to pinpoint that voice over the rest of the manufactured noise we have spent our lives tuning in to. When we recognize and acknowledge those special moments of deeper connection, we can pay homage to the mystery and remember that we are not the center of the universe, but neither are we alone within it. We are part of reality.

If we think of ourselves as fortresses, we can see that each day, we are invaded by manufactured signals and attacks on our psyche. We are exhausted with the struggle, yet we can't run from ourselves. So many of the messages we receive speak directly against balance in our lives. In fact, these messages make us prisoners of addiction. Addiction is an important word; for many of us, it conjures up extreme images: the alcoholic, the meth abuser, the gambler. But it becomes significant for all of us to relearn this term as a label for imbalance in our lives.

Let's go back to the image of the fortress. When the fortress of you is attacked, you feel the anxiety of imbalance—be it emotional, spiritual, financial, or romantic—and you may seek to resolve those feelings by reacting defensively. So, when we are insecure, we lash out at others. When our feelings overwhelm us because we can't process them, we numb them. We buy products, wear masks, and fill the pockets of our oppressors, and they use those funds to create louder messages, all in order to keep us strangers to ourselves. We fall prey to these messages, and, though we know they are unhealthy, like addicts we repeat the patterns of instant gratification and constant dissatisfaction, contributing to the ever-widening imbalance in our lives.

By obeying the wrong external messages, we often try to treat our anxiety with products or chemicals that either don't help, intensify the problem, or create new, lateral problems. The real solution is to directly address the initial cause of our imbalance and restore equilibrium. We are living fraudulent lives because we don't take the time to learn our own stories; I need to keep reiterating the point that reawakening is a process that will continue throughout your entire life. The deficit—the hunger, the lack of connection, call it what you will—is part of the human condition. It creates the path to addiction to the material world and a false sense of time. These patterns nest within our minds. Being largely subliminal, they are so hard to perceive, and the challenge of our life is to move past them.

But in order to restore balance in your life through listening, you must also try to keep moving forward, carrying your foundation with you. Basically, addiction is the need to run. Addiction is what happens when our lives are so out of balance, we succumb to the urge to run from our own self into further imbalance and estrangement. It is a fruitless mission. What you need to be looking for is a sign of life loud enough to wake you up and clear the haze so you can get home to the universe within.

Being diagnosed with Hodgkin's was a profound moment for me. When I was suddenly and unexpectedly confronted with my own mortality, it opened a moment of absolute stillness and silence. In that sudden and infinite moment, I was only aware of the sound of my own heart and my own breath. And there was an audacious invitation to reboot myself, in the absence of all the noise, to listen more deeply. I became aware of what has always been present yet mostly ignored. A need to restore a true meaning in my life thundered in the silence. And it became profoundly apparent that so many of the messages I usually turned to for comfort could not truly save me in a moment like this one. I had to take a leap into the unknown and save my own life.

One of the surprise side effects of my diagnosis was learning all about health insurance. Being able to process life-changing events while still seeking and finding new directions to explore is what I mean by listening and being open. Out of both circumstance and necessity, I was guided in a new direction. I learned so well that I began to support groups and individuals in navigating the treacherous waters, and then I built this support into a business to help employers better sustain the health of their employees, while also saving them money. I realized that much of the cost of insurance could be curtailed by shifting the economic model, through building a foundation of knowledge and personal ownership of wellness and the health insurance system.

Through the following years, I tested and documented the success of this work, believing purchases of plans for organizations would arrive in droves. Instead, even now, I continue to witness how our broken model endures in the face of escalating costs and little health support. I've queried folks as to why they'd support a model that goes against their vested interests, making others wealthy and doing little for their well-being on so many levels. Fear of change is the inevitable response, the reason for maintaining the status quo.

But rather than the change itself, it is the middle, the dark void from the old to the new, where we can get stuck, and that is what we should fear. There, stuck in the middle, is where all the fears congregate, all the "what ifs" that block us. At the same time, this is the place where extraordinary juice, vigor, and creative impulses live, the stuff that propels us to the new. This is the place of hope. The cycle of distraction is no longer enough. This is your life. It is time to go deeper.

As we develop our practice of listening, let's start with a basic question: How do I know when I am conscious? This almost sounds like a silly question at first, right? It's actually a very important question when you consider how much of our time we spend awake, but not aware, trudging along on autopilot with many of our faculties unengaged. We spend so much of our time this way, in fact, that many of us may be truly unaware of an alternative frame of consciousness.

To explore what I mean, I want you to set aside a few moments to take some deep breaths. Focus on that breathing. Then, shift the placement of attention to your solar plexus. Remain aware of your breath. We're not running. We are not retreating. We are present. Sense your body. Feel your breath. Be present. Don't run from your thoughts. That is a misconception about meditation. Rather, set your thoughts free. See what settles and what tugs. Imagine yourself as a great knotted ball as those knots begin to loosen, organically, not pushed, in this place beyond stress. As the philosopher Red Hawk wrote, "The struggle for presence creates attention...being consciously vulnerable develops Love."

When engaged in this exercise for a few minutes, you will notice a shift. This is *not* how we spend most of our time. Most of our time we spend distracted, seeking further distraction, and our gaze is scattered, like buckshot. We are unaware of the many processes of our body, unaware of the desires and hungers that occupy the spaces we are disconnected from. This makes us very vulnerable to manipulation.

The way to return to a more natural place is by making space for liminal time, a concept I have mentioned before. Liminal time is not some sort of science fiction technology. Rather, it is a state of mind, an alternative consciousness, cultivated through meditation, where we loosen our grasp on the ego's boundaries of perception and can dissolve the anxiety that characterizes our man-made, fabricated selves. Entering a liminal time opens us to experiencing a deeper, softer, more fluid form of reality, as well as being present for its offered wisdom.

Liminal time, through a path cleared by meditation, is the place where we dig deeper and call in something bigger than ourselves. This is where we can ask with all of our inner being for some creative, universal intelligence and energy to hold us up, guide us, give us space, and keep us open to the new. Liminal time is a silent place where we can listen.

If I didn't listen to hope, and if I didn't learn to access a greater voice, then maybe I would actually have listened to the doctor when

I was sitting in that small hospital cubicle in the basement with no windows, the stench of death all around me, and the doctor sat four feet away and said, "You are going to die." Maybe I would have ignored my inner voice. And maybe I wouldn't be here, writing these words to you.

As we each sit in our own equivalents of that hospital room, we are bombarded by others' stories, dreams, and plans, and we let them enter our space. If we are in a place of vulnerability, unknowing of who we are and perhaps not in touch with our relationship to our own *beingness*, we might actually say, "Okay, I am going to die," or let them dictate some equally important "truth" for us. However, we always have a choice. One choice is to die. Another choice is to say, "Maybe not today. I will die, but in the meantime I am a *being*; I have hope that I can actually do or become something, so I will not die today."

The point here is that we always have a choice in how we listen. The best way to listen is to return often to a place of inner quiet and pay attention to what resonates within us, and let it lead us forward. The way we know that moment of resonance is that it feels light, like an Aha! goes through our entire being. We all get such moments of opportunity to shift direction, and too many of us pass them by as if they don't matter and have nothing to offer us. But they do. Those Aha! moments that pierce the silence are the gifts that come from the sacred to help guide us. If we learn to listen and pay attention, guidance will come. These sacred gifts are there, and we are there with them as well.

The process of listening is more than simply reclaiming our own stories. When we truly listen, we delve into the space where our own inner voices collide with the divine. A deeper understanding and guidance awaits us there, in that space, enabling us to move forward on our healing journeys.

In the previous chapter, "Opening," we talked about recognizing divinity within ourselves and others. Now I am asking you to listen to and follow that sacred divinity. Life is full of learning opportunities. Often we don't see the forest for the trees. But we are provided with the evidence and connections of a bigger picture everywhere, if we just look and listen. This world is turned by cosmic laws and connections, each event fueling the significance of the next. When we move beyond defining our reality by our momentary reactions, we learn to listen to this deeper message.

For example, on my last visit to New York City with my second wife and her son, I promised him the sort of legendary hot dogs and pizza one can only find in New York City. We went to the last remaining kosher deli on Second Avenue, where pickles and chocolate soda were brought to tables before orders were even placed. My stepson drank all three glasses and even ordered a larger glass to wash down his hot dog.

After we ate, I requested hot water for the digestive herbal tea I'd brought with me. After it was brought and I drank my tea, the manager arrived at the table asking if I knew what I had done. She went on to let me know, just in case I was unaware, that she would need to throw out the cup and silverware I had used, as this was a kosher restaurant. Never mind that herbs are by nature kosher; in her mind, I was the cause of her breaking a commandment.

My days of being scolded in Hebrew school flooded back, and I left the deli shaking. We moved on to the Empire State Building, so that my wife and stepson could go to the top. Since I'd made that trip numerous times, I decided to stay below, feeling the need to chill out after the scalding reprimand over my herbal tea.

In a short while, a cavalcade of police on motorcycles poured down Fifth Avenue, followed by vehicles of many sizes and shapes with electrified menorahs on their roofs. While I sat, holding up the building and struggling to calm my nerves, a bearded smiling face called to me from a minivan stopped on the street. This was New York City, so the sidewalks were packed with people, and yet, out of the crowd, he beckoned to me.

I knew he was the rebbe, or rabbi, so I went to the vehicle, and he said with his Eastern European accent, "What is your name?"

I said my Hebrew name, Asher, and he asked where I was from.

"Oregon," I said.

"Oy," he said. "So far away. Do you have a menorah?"

I said no, and he handed me a box holding a new menorah.

"Do you have candles?" he asked.

No, I said, I didn't have a menorah, so I didn't have candles. Of course, the candles appeared next from the back of the vehicle, and I took them reverently. We smiled. He grabbed my head and blessed me. They were sacred gifts in a moment of hope, indeed.

When my family came out of the front door from their experience at the top of the Empire State Building, I was delighted to inform them that all was good with God and the herbal tea incident was redeemed. And yet, the meeting with the rebbe was so much sweeter because of the anxiety and shame that preceded it—just as spring is so much more vibrant following the winter. I realized that I had once again allowed another voice, one of scorn, to deflate my own. In that kosher restaurant, I became a child again. But the rebbe reminded me of the divinity within me. And thankfully, I listened.

We must ask ourselves: Am I being present at every moment in my life, so that I make room for the gifts and the teaching, the love and the guidance? So that I can have these connections, these relationships in those moments I feel the most separate?

When I attended my first Quaker worship, it was out of curiosity aroused by a group of people and their faith. They wanted to support others' journeys without the need to interfere with how that person listened inwardly. The service had no books or hymnals, and there were no symbols to break my attention. There were no leaders and no words to recite. I sat, uncomfortably at first, listening to whatever came into my consciousness. Eventually, in the listening, I heard hundreds of years of other voices: individually quiet, yet together. The meeting-house was the repository of the quiet power of the human. I felt the power of togetherness and of silence. The Quakers honor divinity so much that they will not tell you who you are or what you believe.

———

When I was told by the doctor that the cancer had made its way to my lungs, and I responded that in my own meditations I saw my lungs were pink, the medical community said I was crazy, that there was no way I could see my lungs. How was I, the patient, able to see something when technology got a completely different interpretation?

I saw something different because I stayed in a place of connection with something greater. It wasn't just me looking at me, it was me opening through meditative prayer, being able to see at a level that maybe I couldn't see before. Hope doesn't arrive because we sit there and expect it to lift us up and take us somewhere new. Hope comes because we listen and open ourselves to some magic, even if just for an instant.

When I first got married, I was young. Even after almost a quarter century with my first wife, I still didn't fully comprehend all of the dynamics of the different levels of love, relationship, and partnership. After our divorce, it was in that liminal space of being quiet and open that my poetry started to come, at two o'clock in the morning. In the wee hours, I was being awakened by a muse, and I kept asking, "Can't you come at three in the afternoon?"

But it kept coming in the middle of the night, so I knew I needed to get a pad of paper and a pen. Listening is asking, not commanding. In those moments, I began to go to a place inside of me that was deeper than I'd ever gone, and a new understanding of myself emerged. I'd never before seen myself as a poet. I'd spent most of my life creating new forms, structures, and institutions for others and their journeys. Now I was being asked to make a leap into looking at myself in a way that was radically new and to call myself something different—Poet—a person who listens and speaks rhythmically and as concisely as possible, with statements that impact each listener or reader through their beauty. Eventually I realized that the poetry was speaking to me as answers to the prayers and questions I'd asked. I was being called to acknowledge and translate these answers through the muse, and now, as I share my answers with you, I also call on you to solicit and translate your own answers.

After some self-discovery and healing, I opened again to the prospect of relationship, and in walked a new partner. For a while, we met and helped each other grow. We made a covenant to work on our relationship together and to stay in the work as long as we could. However, that relationship ended as well. And I followed my conditioned instincts back into that familiar place of darkness and uncertainty.

Did I fail at life? Of course not. As I have said before, there is no microwave solution to the challenges of our lives. Life is a series of interconnected cycles. There is the search and desire for something more, which calls to us and motivates us. And there are the inevitable backslides. This is healthy.

So, what do we hold on to when the struggle or darkness or confusion returns? We return to ourselves. We gain the understanding that magic is always available, that the opportunity to listen is always there. We remind ourselves that our anxiety and addictive tendency to run away is something we have learned and practiced our whole lives, and we must proactively pursue the deeper truths we know exist within us that connect us to one another and to ourselves.

PRACTICE

Sit or stand, or if you aren't in the right space, take a walk somewhere quiet. Breathe and keep breathing till your breath slows to a rhythmic pace of gentleness.

See yourself as writer and director of a story that affirms.

Where do you go, where do you see yourself when you are most at peace? You'll know this place as your breathing remains gentle.

If your focus starts to falter and you feel like you're tripping in a hole, find another place. Go to that place daily. If possible, start by going to this magical place at the same time each day. Make this an empowered part of your routine. Prioritize it.

See what is waiting for you. Act from a place of listening, paying attention to the wisdom of the voice inside, rather than the crowd. How does it feel to begin to trust your guidance, even if and when it's contrary to what you were always told?

Learn discernment. Don't be afraid to stumble along the way. Summon your faith to deepen your exploration. Feel the power of your connection. After a while, you will find a way to arrive at this place of listening or to drop in at other times.

As you're breathing, say words that affirm your story, your life. Remember your words or write them down. You're the author. The story will continue to unfold and the script will develop. Ask yourself how the script can lead you to grow and lead you to love.

By listening, you will find trust and guidance. Let this inner guidance overcome material compulsion in your life.

ANOTHER DAY

Well, the sky is still blue;
Another day
Has made its appearance,
And I have no choice
But to remain open
To the journey.
And, if I want,
I can do it even believing
I am in control
If that makes me feel better.
Just so long as I remember
That's just another myth
Among many
To see another blue sky.
Still, quieting to hear
God's direction
Could lessen the discomfort.
But who knows?
It could all be illusion.
Except this one
Brings me to grace—as though the path
Was marked by the Divine.

LISTEN

Shema, listen:
Treasures from the deep
Made their appearance today.
They were sunk a time ago,
Yet they signaled me
To pay attention.
Shema, listen
As though God
Said it was time for love
To come to us
If we would only hear
The other blessed.
A treasure came to me
Because I heard the call
Of the other singing,
Of angels and cherubim
Entering our core,
Sending the colors and light
To fill our souls,
To awaken our hearts.
Shema, I listened
And received
The blessing
To meet true love.
Today I met you
And was born anew.

DID I EVER PAY ATTENTION

Life come and goes
With its own calendar,
Yet I can't seem to abide
Moving at a pace
That forces me in an unnatural way.
Where did my patience go?
Did I ever pay attention
At all,
Or do I think God's timetable
Is for all but me?
And so moving, or
Pushing, so that Life herself
Will stand up and listen,
Stopping all else,
Listening to only me
While other crises wait for theirs.
It is I,
The center of the universe,
Impatient; maybe a little scared
To take the time
To see we are here
For all,
And Life asks for us
To share
So we'll all be heard.

A HEART CAN HURT

A heart can hurt
If you're in touch
With who you are
As you struggle
In this world
To cross the boundaries,
Checking in as though you care.
A heart will hurt
Because you care,
But the pain shows
That you're alive,
And however deep
The hurt is felt,
It's better
Than feeling nothing at all.

A heart beats,
Announcing regularly
If you only listen:
Take the time;
Love someone.
A chance may come
To feel alive
And share in joy
If you can give
As well as take.
To love fully
Is to feel and know;
It is in the paradox
Where we are home,
Open to the wonder
And comfort in the glow.

THE FEARS I'VE BEEN HOLDING

And now the shaking
I've been feeling
For most of my life
Has made its way
To my physical truth;
The fears I've been holding
Have now appeared
In my pores,
For I have squelched
The passions
Of my soul
Until almost too late.
I opened, though,
And there's no
Shutting down again.
So in the lonely,
Disturbing place of my life,
It finally made its way to my
Body
So I can know
It's time to challenge
The patterns of a life
Not yet whole.

PLAY THE GAME

Can't find love being you—
Or so you think.
And you don't know how to
Play the game
When she says
She wants a sensitive man
Who nurtures and cares
And knows how to share,
Who also is strong
In the most appropriate way.

So you change your story
And become a stranger to you
To find your mate.
And as time goes by,
You lose your soul.
So you found your mate
And lost your soul,
So wounded you don't even know,
So lost you can't find home.

And then it tumbles
And falls to the ground
Alone again
With the stranger in you.
Where to look
To find yourself?
It's been too long,
And the pain is too far down.
But you can come home,
And home you must come
Before it happens again,
As it did many times before.

ALLOW

This time it's your daughter,
Or it could be your son,
And it feels somehow
Worse
Than when it was you.
But how did she get it
At the age of twenty-four,
Or any age at all?
How does a god
Allow
A tender child,
Whose only purpose here
Is to spread beauty
For the world to know
It's whole—
Not that it has any meaning now,
Or ever did.
Did I pass it on, and
How did it come to me?
Or really,
Maybe the wonder
Is all there is,
And in life's plan
Is the opportunity to touch
When touching was so hard;
To know self and the other
When opportunities were missed.
Maybe it's a million things,
And some may even be true,
But all we can know
Is love.

And when life comes
And interrupts the story,
It helps to know we can.

A SYSTEM OF HEALTH

How do you
Have a system of health
When touch and care
Are replaced with categories
Of things
Named and unnamed
To separate
And create fear?
How do we heal
When love is not covered
And no test can touch—
And if it did,
The surprise would be
Too great to bear?
We are crying in silence
Or aloud:
Hold me,
Comfort me,
So I can do it for you.
Don't be detached, and
Don't observe.
You are in my life;
We are each other,
And healing is love.
Just listen.
Just care,
For we are here
To guide our way home.

WHERE IS GOD

Where is God
When the crisis comes?
I created him in my image
To be here in time of need.
I created him to come
When I called.
Oh God, so big and strong,
Guardian and protector of my being;
It hurts too far down—
Even you can't reach the pain.
I would have created
You differently if only I knew
That life could be this cruel,
And then so lovely,
And then another…
It's the dark and then
The light.
It's the way it comes
When you planned
For another—
God.
I need to rethink you.

YOU'RE RUNNING AWAY

Slow down your emotions;
Love will come in its own time.
You've prepared for a lifetime,
Meeting yourself through
All the pains and joys.
But how do you take
It slow
When a connection
Is made so deep
In your core?
You're running away
And don't know where,
As though you're in a maze,
As though all reason has gone away.
Do your best
To be at home, at rest,
For no one knows.
Believe in the wonder
And awe
Of life.
Not many can pass
Through fear,
But when we do,
Our soul can love
Being home where we belong.

CAN YOU HEAR

Can you hear joy?
Or has it been so long
The pain has greeted
Your every day,
Waking to arise
Only to hear,
"What's wrong?"
Each and every day
Instead of "Good morning;
Go out and have a wondrous day."

Can you bring in joy?
You really are divine
And born to find wonder.
The new day can be a birth,
A miracle for us all.
Accept your gift.
Pass it on,
For in the sharing
We all come home
To the long deep breath
Of calm,
Enveloping love.

CHAPTER FIVE

Uniting

All touch is of great consequence.

REV. DR. ROBERT "BOB" KIMBALL

UNION

Are you there—
Or rather here, beside me?
Am I feeling the touch of togetherness
Or just dreaming of belonging?
You are so illusive;
My heart wanders in its insecurities so
That I pretend to be alone
When you are just a touch away,
Reaching for my hand
Without the words.
We are one.
Amen.

REMEMBERING OUR BEGINNING, OUR UNION WITH THE DIVINE AND our fellow humankind, is essential to healing and wholeness. While *opening* is about creating an I-Thou contract with the Divine, *uniting* is about getting in touch with your shared humanity. It's about a community working together for the greater good. Together, these ideas and practices show us how to unite. When everyone's individual gifts are pooled together in unity, communities can have extraordinary power.

More and more, we are moving past the philosophical lessons of this book and into the practice portions. Don't let that scare you. You started this journey because you wanted change, and that's where you are headed. We have looked at reclaiming and proclaiming ourselves. We have learned to honor and discern the voice of divinity within ourselves and our neighbor. Now we come to the point of action. The clearest way to honor the direction we have been seeking is to unite in meaningful, productive communities in order to accomplish the goals our hearts call us to.

Our lives come from one original source. We aren't separate from this source, this light, this divinity. We are one with it. Science and spiritual teachings are converging on this concept today. What traditionally has been scoffed at as "spiritualism" is being viewed today as a reality of physics. The Kabbalistic source, the Zohar, puts it this way:

> A blinding spark flashed
> Within the concealed of the concealed,
> From the mystery of the Infinite,
> A cluster of vapor in formlessness
> Under the impact of breaking through,

On high and hidden point shown.
Beyond that point nothing is known.
So it is called Beginning.

Once we become awakened, listening to our purpose and finding authentic meaning in our lives, it is easy to lapse into the egotistic notion of believing we've found all the answers. The Divine has smacked our butt and sent us on our way. This is the most important time to remember that the same divinity exists in everyone else, too, and has shown different pieces of a whole, infinite truth to each of us. Each of us alone is finite, lacking the resources to process that infinite wisdom. And so, we are given the gift of each other. Union involves the energy and effort of the collective.

When we looked at the second step in the healing process, proclaiming, we learned how to connect and embolden ourselves through proclaiming our truths. Now we will merge that skill with our newfound ability to listen and connect so that we may fulfill our life's purpose. When bringing your clarified selfhood to the collective *we*, you must learn *how* to assimilate without dominating, controlling, or judging so the group can create something glorious beyond each individual's own limitations. This synthesis creates a realm of love where listening, opening, and directed fluidity may occur.

The practice of uniting overcomes the arrogance of singular-perspective monopolizations of the truth. The "I" is the stick in the eye we must remove to see clearly before acting. We have spent a lot of time focusing on the inner covenants we make, but we must also remember the lesson of the shared life. As in all things, we must find balance in order to heal fully. At every step in this process, your ego has a strategy to regain control, and you must temper it with mindfulness of the common good. Are we open to wonder? When we are looking for God, the greatest clues we are given to help us work on the mystery are others engaged in their own searches. This drive to unite has always driven me, and through practice, I have learned to refine it and bloom.

Let me give you an example. While in college in the late sixties, I was given the gift of being included in a collective of extraordinary people. To this day, I still feel profound connection with the men and women who were with me in this powerful group: Bruce, Tom, Betty, and Debra. Bruce and I were undergrads and best friends who did everything together. Tom and I met doing an internship at Community Improvement Through Youth, Inc. (CITY), in the District of Columbia. He was getting a master's degree in urban affairs, while I was finishing my bachelor's. Betty and Debra were deeply thoughtful women who both practiced transcendental meditation. We were young and radical, and it was a radical time, and most important, we hung in together. I was probably the wildest of the bunch.

Initially I was studying city management and urban affairs in college, with the idea of developing cities along earlier models, where community squares were important spaces for social exchange—not just for commerce but for community—places where people could come together. In Europe, the town squares, the piazzas, and the plazas are still central meeting places, with cafés and music, art and conversation and movement, and people still meet in these gathering places.

I was greatly influenced by America's New England towns in the original formation of our country, which had the center greens, with the steepled church on one side and the shops on the other. This seemed to me to follow the ancient Greek concept of the agora. It's funny how the wisdom of cycles, in the microcosm of our lives and the macrocosm of history, is so persistent! Even in my professional education, I was pursuing a spiritual quest, which others had trod before me, and it was leading me in a new direction.

Tom and I proposed the original idea, bringing the concept to our favorite professor, Bernie. Our goal was to place students in internships in community-based groups working on the streets of DC, versus typical placements in governmental agencies. A supportive and extraordinary man, Bernie liked our idea and agreed to become our mentor, muse, and more.

Here we were, in our late teens and early twenties, proposing to a university that we could place their students among entrenched community groups and lead them to a new theoretical and practical experience. This was a chance for students to really be out there, engaged in the real world, doing good both for themselves and for the community. We united in what we created—sometimes without a clear sense of knowing our path, closer to the Buddhist notion of *not* knowing, but moving toward knowing. With openness, we surrendered to the whole. The five of us in our group were from vastly different backgrounds, had different skill sets, and, as many of our meetings showed, were raised in different belief systems. And yet, we all gave ourselves permission to be with one another in a way that we'd never known we had the capacity to do. In that surrender, we found merged capabilities that can only be described as sacred.

Through the generous gift of one urban affairs professor, we started with students from American University, and within a couple of years, we also began programs at other DC colleges. With the foundation's funding, as well as funds from the colleges, we were able to place students with powerful groups in need, while we gave them the support of structure and classes.

We were young and in many ways naïve and idealistic, but we were able to play in the big leagues at major universities and do some of the most important work of our lives. We walked into foundations and the executive director would look at us with an eyebrow raised and say, "What are you up to now?" And then he'd often give us a small grant to get that new project moving. It was an exhilarating time in my life.

Our unit operated as a cooperative; that is, we reached consensus by emphasizing the needs and perspectives of the collective. We found wisdom in many diverse religious groups, such as Quakers, Catholic workers, and Eastern religious practitioners. We each brought our own histories, personalities, and ideas to the project, but we made a covenant with each other to work together, fulfill our commitments, and uphold our word. We united! Sometimes, in fulfilling our covenant, we argued intensely before coming to a collective decision, and at other times, we peacefully agreed almost instantaneously, like devout disciples at a Quaker meeting. Either way, I could never have accomplished all that we did alone, and I have never found this type of group again.

As young radicals, we weren't always graceful in our interactions. Bruce and I were often in a playful space, debating with each other on various topics. Betty and Tom were most often the ones keeping us in line. Still, anytime we disagreed, we didn't let that drive us apart. When an argument arose, Tom, Bruce, or Betty might say, "I completely disagree with what you're saying, but let's get into it."

Together we shared our gifts and made the impossible possible. In our union, work and play, joys and sorrows were never separated. That is one of the greatest secrets we can learn: when we connect to the divinity within ourselves, it fills us with a hunger to connect with the divinity in others. We were doing all this together; it was a journey that allowed us to share our lives and to care about what was happening with the students and community groups we served.

Fifty-some years later, these folks are still my closest friends and confidants. One of the things I stumble over sometimes is that I haven't been able to find the exact magic of this kind of union again. I will always be looking for it and hoping others out there, who may be looking for me, won't give up until we find one another.

My heart longs for sacred collaborating, and so, in a place of hope, I remain open to it. Together, we said yes, and we still say yes, even when the world says no. I think the work is to just keep saying yes, no matter how hard it seems.

Through my union with others, I have learned to discern what I might find in others that is valuable to my quest. Intention truly attracts. In the openness of hope, I recently found a spiritual direction training program in Portland. My spiritual director was a highly progressive nun named Mary Ann. She has energy similar to my old friend Tom: completely open and joyful. As with Tom, I trust her completely and share with her things I haven't otherwise spoken of in years.

During our most recent meeting, as we sat together, she said to me, "Arnie, I grow with you."

I responded, "And I grow with you." I meant that, and I mean it more and more every time I see her. When we see each other, we just smile. Our energy centers each other. And in this practice of our friendship, the preciousness of time to be fully present in the now reveals itself. We're a gift to each other, and we live in the moment, with no distractions, in a constantly evolving unity. Isn't this unity in the now a wonderful lens to see life through? Uniting adds a dimension to my place in this world by reminding me of the well of meaning we all draw from. And the realization of our shared power empowers me to act.

When we create barriers in our lives to make sure that we remain separate and categorized, when we don't open ourselves to the possibility of growing with each other, we are only half alive—part of us remains dormant. The purpose of proclaiming is not to define the boundaries around ourselves but to begin the process of opening, of enlarging our boundaries to include as much love as possible. Meaningful union helps us rise above ourselves, allowing us to grow through our shared divinity.

As we learn about our value in the world, we must internalize that it is a *shared* value. I believe that separation and disconnection cause our lack of awareness of our shared value, and they are also the reason our health care system in the United States struggles. So, I continue to ask, in terms of health care and everything else: Can we develop a model to support our communities in a healing embrace? Can we make ourselves whole together? If our society and its various institutions and infrastructures do not represent the realities of our connection, what can we do to fix them?

We must start by modeling that different reality. Union can only occur when we've done the work of identifying and reclaiming ourselves, proclaiming that identity to society, opening ourselves to the I-Thou covenant, and listening to the divinity within all of us. We must move beyond the need to use one another by realizing that we are sharing the same essence. That is a powerful paradigm shift in how we relate to one another.

How do you treat your family? How would you treat a stranger if you realized they were your family? One of the most profound spiritual realizations you can internalize is that we ARE all family. We are one. If you change your life accordingly and live up to the implications of that great truth, nothing can stop you.

All of this transformation is possible when we come from a place of love and grace, without putting our beliefs on someone else, and meet in the clearly identifiable center, from which the spokes of the wheel emerge, as Martin Buber suggested. In the case of CITY, the five of us were the spokes of a proverbial wheel, held by a clear message of union at the center. Finding strength in each other's differences, we were able to bring union to the universities, the communities, and to each other.

Healing occurs when we open up from being a clear self to an I-Thou, which is itself a sacred whole and also a valuable, unique part of something greater. Here in these pages, we celebrate and honor this fluidity, the reciprocity of union and the wholeness of the wheel that takes place when we flow in the dance of the I-Thou.

Doctors live their lives by the Hippocratic Oath: "First, do no harm." What oath do you live by, and how does it affect your interactions with the rest of us? How do your interactions with the rest of us affect your purpose? What are you passionate about? What new priorities have you picked up through this contemplative process? What do you feel compelled to try or do?

PRACTICE

These are great questions, but your practice today is to put this book down. The lesson of uniting cannot be internalized through reading, thinking, meditating, or praying. Now it is time to act. I want you to take a chance. Move beyond what you perceive your comfort zone to be and find someone to engage with in the pursuit of what matters to you. Engage. This activity won't always be easy. But it will open you up to the wonder of this world we share, and I promise you will learn from it and derive energy from it. My hope is that you will form a great union and accomplish something that matters.

HOLD ON

Hold on—
For even as the waves appear,
Some are to fill your heart
With joy,
Remembering days of long ago
That are yours.
See them
Dancing under the stars;
See them
Laughing playfully,
Silly and all.

Hold on—
They came to keep you warm
On those long,
Cold, and lonely nights and days;
You are not alone.

PAY ATTENTION

Life asks only to be tended;
To pay attention
So it won't go wild
With thoughts of fear,
And its beauty disappear.

Life only asks to touch.
Even if the fingers do the probing,
It's the heart
That guides its course.

Life only asks that we heal time
So pleasure is at home
Once again;
Our desire is a new mistress
Awaiting our return.

And so life only asks
For us to quiet and love,
To make home warm and aglow,
That we choose to be
With one another
And individually, but not alone.
Life asks for an embrace
To soften and make whole.
Life asks for it all
And will take nothing less.

OPEN BEYOND

I cry at the sight
Of lovers
Touching each other,
Forgetting who they are
For the moment,
Or however long.

I open beyond my place
Of fear
When the other
Shares their inner truth,
Allowing touch
To come in,
Engulfing
My every breath.

For it is in these
Rare and liminal
Moments
That I know I
Am human, and I know
Why God
Bestowed blessings
And chose us to appear
In seven days of
Creation.

TAKE ME AWAY

Take me away
On a long ride
Into that place
Of mystery and awe.
I need to sail into
The waters with its
Expansive and wondrous
Tides,
To go along
Following the natural
Way.
Come, God has a plan—
It is all okay.
Just hold on;
Surrender into the uncharted
Yet welcoming waters.
You may just connect
With your inner nature
And the rhythms of earth's embrace.

LOOK INTO MY HEART

Look into my heart;
What do you see?
A soul so large it
Wants to serve the world.
A heart that believes
There is a right and wrong,
Yet understands there is
The gray spectrum in life.
We are here to serve and love;
We are here to take care
And be taken care of.
Service is meant to be shared,
For in the giving we become one.
We learn to move beyond
The singular ego
And into the truth of self.
Through giving we learn
We live in an abundant universe
That flourishes with each gift we make.

COME IN, COME IN

Come in, come in!
I've been waiting
for you.
You've taken your time,
But no matter.
You're here.
You say
You thought we didn't exist—
Only in your dreams.
So are you awake now?
And how does it feel?
Real is where you are
At the time you choose.
So welcome again;
You're awake if you feel
And journey with the Other.
Together we find home,
The natural state of your being.
Come; we'll go together.
Sharing makes it real
Somehow.
So it's you for now;
Enjoy down deep
Where feelings are home.
Stay for a while till
You awake anew.

CHAPTER SIX

Meeting

It matters not how strait the gate,
How charged with punishments the scroll,
I am the master of my fate,
I am the captain of my soul.

WILLIAM ERNEST HENLEY

OPENING OUR HEARTS

I know that walking
On either extreme
Leads me into realms of suffering.
Yet I seem to drift
Too many times—
Sometimes I'm asleep, or
Even while awake,
And it takes vigilance
To be mindful
And find the middle way.
I ask for Your help
To guide me gently
And with love.
I know I use my free will,
But I also need your wisdom
And compassion.
Together it's easier
For both to know the way.
Amen.

OUR STRANGERS ARE THE TRUEST VERSION OF OURSELVES, THE merged manifestation of the qualities of the heart we have been contemplating. In our lives, we are the thread that connects them. It is time to fully meet our Strangers, and this is an invitation to reflect again on the I-Thou relationship. Our Strangers are the truths we hold within ourselves, as well as the articulated connection that tethers us to divinity and the shared spark that unites and connects us with every person we meet.

Our Strangers are who we were before society stripped us down and split us psyches. We must allow our Strangers to be our guides through the wilderness of our society and back to wellness. Once we realize that we, the Divine, and our neighbors are one and the same in this journey, we will no longer see ourselves as an adversary blocking our own path. Conflict will no longer consume us. Emotions become useful tools again, instead of mutineers fighting to dominate our lives and dictate our realities. Recognizing ourselves in others and seeing the divinity that shines through us will free us from illusions of control and the cycle of anxiety that illusion demands. But meeting our Strangers also puts us face to face with our oldest adversary: ego.

The key element we must continue to examine is ego—not because it is so important to our identities but because its influence is so deceptive. Again: we are *not* our egos; it is only a part of how our real selves identify within this world. But the weight of significance we often mistakenly ascribe to the ego masks the path to those other, more significant connections.

When we are in balance, the ego serves the whole. Does your ego serve you? Do you have a healthy relationship with your ego? To answer these questions, it might be helpful to think of how animals behave in the wild. When a wild animal is sick or wounded, its instinct is to hide its pain so it doesn't seem vulnerable—an instinct that serves the animal's best chance of survival in its environment.

Often we can observe house pets exhibiting these same behaviors of masking vulnerability. However, in a different environment, the instinct no longer serves the animal. When aid, love, and solutions are offered, humans can make a choice that wild animals cannot—we can choose to rebalance ourselves and modify our behaviors to serve our best interests.

Clarity is hard to come by in a society where so often the most ardent religious leaders and politicians seem most prone to scandal, even while pitching their warped, hypocritical values. Adultery is okay, as long as you aren't gay. Murder is okay, as long as it's done by your tax dollars instead of your hands. Child labor is okay, as long as you don't actually see it and it saves you five bucks on a sweater. Society wants us to believe that we deserve whatever we want and, if we simply ignore the consequences and find an adequate scapegoat, there should be a way to bend the facts to our will. Yet, at some point, so many of us find ourselves sleepless at night, continuing to wonder why…those are our Strangers, trying to remind us who we really are.

For the same reason you wouldn't build a house on shifting sands, you can't create a foundation for your life based on ego and emotion. Emotions and desire are fleeting and subjective—as such, they are unreliable narrators. And emotions are much easier for others to manipulate than, say, hard logic or a consistent moral compass, because these are built on and strengthened by self-clarity and honoring our deeper connections.

Ego works in a devious and manipulative way, inviting us to mask our own vulnerabilities and imbalances from ourselves. The shallow, easily flattered ego is comforted, like a child with a lollipop, by easy answers and keeps us from seeking the more difficult answers that nourish the soul. The ego does not want us to see ourselves clearly in a way that allows us to seek healing.

All the things I want you to try—reclaiming, proclaiming, opening, listening, uniting, meeting—are allies of the soul, not the ego. We need to master our egos rather than be dominated by them. It is time to meet our Strangers. Ultimately, we complete the circuit connecting our souls to the world. You have come to this place from your desire to transcend imbalance. Have you gotten in touch with yourself and your stories so that you can meet another person without fear or ego getting in the way? Have you learned to see your own bullshit with clarity and get out of your own way? For healing to take place, relationally, we must come intentionally to the Thou. Each of us must ask: Am I receptive to being present and allowing even challenging ideas and thoughts without making judgments or having to own everything? Can I be present with others while also standing with my own truth in a place of proclaiming who I am?

At this point, some of these questions might seem like a review, and in a sense, they are. As we take each step forward, our perception grows and shifts. Now that you are merging your previous steps to see the connective whole, it is prudent to keep one eye looking backward, as it were, so you can see how some of your previous answers and practices might be shifting as you build on a new, stronger foundation of reality.

What many of us think is reality is the illusion, the mask. I'm not implying that we're in the Matrix or something, but perhaps the comparison will help you see what I mean. The context we live in, and what we build upon, is an illusion compared to what I want to dig down to—the deeper reality of our Strangers. Many people think they can go right to the heart of an idea before they've really gotten to a strong place of knowing who they are or understanding an idea's components. It comes from that microwave mentality of wanting instant gratification rather than having to work for the bounty of commitment and growth. But there's no shortcut to self-revelation. When we try to take a shortcut and avoid the work of soul searching, we're going in weak, and we cannot partner as equals. Food is grown. Air is breathed. Minds are cultivated, strength is gained, and souls are forged in the furnace of our lives. This place of the heart is a shared place, a place of uniting and meeting and infinite openness. And the only way we can share with integrity is by entering that place feeling confident about ourselves and who we are, aware of our purpose.

In this receptive place of heart, we call again on the humility and openness of *faith* and allow our hearts to soften and guide us out of the head and into receptive connection. Our Strangers echo the truth we haven't been ready to hear, but that truth, that reality, isn't foreign. It resonates from within. Embrace it. See how it connects us to living an authentic, meaningful life. We must learn to trust these higher truths and what our deepest self is burning to tell us.

When Deepak Chopra was looking at differences between faith and beliefs, he saw that beliefs can be boundaries, closing us off. We are encouraged, for instance, to hold tightly to religious dogmatic beliefs, because our church, synagogue, parents, family, or friends reward us for holding them and offer disincentives for not holding onto them tightly enough by appealing to our emotions, our fears, and our ego.

Holding a belief tightly means bolstering the notion that you are right, and thus justified in inharmonious action, because you are defining yourself by a generalized hypothetical intention rather than by your reality. The effort of maintaining this mentality and buying into society's deceptive, destructive messages immediately shuts down receptivity and encourages imbalance and hypocrisy, as exhibited daily in our news and public scandals.

But by inviting spaciousness—keeping boundaries open, knowing that whatever perception or opinion we're holding at the moment could very well move into many different configurations—we guarantee that we stay truly receptive. By being receptive and by listening, we engage with the reality that our own hard-earned logic builds. Eventually, adhering to our real values, rather than superstition, provides concrete direction and priorities for us.

If there's something you hold dear and precious, just acknowledge that it *is* precious and important to you. Ask what that might demand of you in response. See what covenant forms and actions you are willing to do to honor what's important to you. But realize at the same time that another's precious thoughts, feelings, culture, and concerns may be equally precious to them, and just as deserving of honor.

In the last few years, I've experienced a lot of loss. About two months ago, I was excitedly planning to visit friends in the

San Francisco Bay Area. One of those was my mentor and sacred friend, Bob. We were continuing our unbroken conversation of over thirty years on the dynamics of human relation. But a month before we were to meet, I received an email from a former classmate and another close student of Bob's that Bob's wife, Lorna, had passed away and that in short order, Bob had followed her. I am still holding the grief, struggling with the loss.

Not knowing what else to do and knowing he couldn't answer, I called Bob's house. When someone picked up, I jumped. One of Bob and Lorna's sons was just leaving the house but felt compelled to answer. We chatted awhile, sharing stories about his dad, and he invited me to a family celebration event of their lives. The gathering was to be held at a Vietnamese restaurant on the water near Bob and Lorna's house, where they dined during the last couple of years. The family owners of the restaurant wanted to hold and cater a loving celebration for them.

This was not the most convenient moment, if I were to define my choices by that notion. But, in the end, I was so grateful to be there, soaking up the love and listening to Bob and Lorna's grandchildren tell stories of the deep and rare foundational love they'd experienced, the gift of feeling blessed by grandparents who lived with complete receptivity, personally and professionally. Both Bob and Lorna had always shown up strong for themselves, ready to share life with others.

Even in grief, I knew I was present to a celebration of wondrous, delicious lives lived fully, characterized by the strength of knowing and the softness of heart, the power and energy of free-flowing receptivity. My Stranger allows me to live beyond fears, grief, and depression and open to my deeper feelings. I am connected to Bob in a way that his death does not alter. I am present in my life and the lives of others and open to the blessings of intimacy. I release myself into this energy. We all have it, and we know from Chinese medicine that this life force, or *chi*, needs to move freely.

Yet we all experience moments of tightness, when we actually obstruct this flow of energy. Some of us are so accustomed to shutting ourselves off, and it is so ingrained in us, that freedom from the tightness and a return to an energetic, natural way of being might even feel foreign. This is partly what I mean by the illusion of context. When pain is so typical, its absence feels foreign. We become warped into unnatural spiritual and emotional states and forget our Stranger, our true values, our real priorities. We are more comfortable using chemicals and substances like caffeine and alcohol to artificially bring ourselves up and back down; we use alcohol and drugs to dull our pain, kick open doors for us, and numb our emotions. We lose touch with the healthy living, spiritual clarity, and receptivity that will restore our cycles naturally.

When you are in an argument or a place of dissension with friends, parents, peers, or life itself, don't you feel that reaction physically? When a test or a deadline looms, when a bill is overdue, or maybe even when the neighbor gets a new car, we react emotionally. And our emotional reactions turn physical and affect our bodies, our breathing, and our health, slowly dominating the way we perceive every aspect of our reality. An unstable emotional foundation manifests itself physically and corrupts the quality of our lives.

I learned so much about the sacredness of these connections when I practiced acupuncture. When someone goes for an acupuncture treatment, the acupuncturist is really just opening the channels of this constriction that we've created so that, in receptivity, we can again gift ourselves with that opening and flow and healing.

Since much of our internal mechanics can be traced back to our families, I'd like to share another story about mine. Some years ago, my family invited us to travel three thousand miles to Florida for Passover. With that invitation came all of my parents' expectations of us arriving in Florida as exactly the people they've always wanted us to be.

On Passover, I brought my niece, nephews, and stepson to the beach before the ceremony and dinner. As the children and I were feeling a Shabbat-like moment, I received a call from my mother, screaming, "Where are you?" and "Get back here immediately!" Even though there was plenty of time, her beliefs about where and how we needed to be introduced tightness and reactiveness into the experience. I fell into an old family pattern and responded to her panic, rushing the children back into the car and ripping us all away from our peaceful, grounding Shabbat experience to race back to my parents' house.

The ceremony began with all of us shaking unnecessarily as my father mumbled his way through. In an attempt to reclaim myself and proclaim my own story, I asked if I could read some of the Haggadah I'd created for the event. My parents met me with resistance, yet others wanted a reprieve, and I could feel their receptivity to the possibility of joy entering the room. I went to the car and brought in my creation, as well as my true self, to share.

I left that trip having learned that if I come to an invitation knowing who I am and stay clear, if I establish and maintain emotional truths that nurture me as I'm in relationship, I will experience these free-flowing moments. I used the quality of proclaiming, but I also learned to be receptive to my own needs in a complex social dynamic while honoring those I experienced it with. Otherwise, if I constantly paid attention to how I'm taking care of others at the expense of my own wellness, I would tiptoe around instead of walking proudly in my life.

Family often presents us with great opportunities to evaluate who we are and how far we've come while further opening our own hearts. We can use our families as mirrors of ourselves in many ways. I'm asking you to expand your scope and deepen those instincts. Everyone is a reflection of you in some ways, just as you are a reflection of your Stranger.

When I choose to accept invitations, I must remain cognizant that I am not there to fulfill false expectations. I'm there to show up as fully Arnie as Arnie can be. Boy, that's sure a paradigm shift, isn't it? While that sometimes might invite what we perceive as conflict, ultimately if you shift your practice to this, you'll find it quite liberating. To be *receptive* means to show up with *hope*, and hopefulness is a place of tenderness. This is how we meet our Stranger. I want to acknowledge the word *tender*, because when we are receptive, we get vulnerable and take risks. Sometimes, the hardest place to show up to as Arnie is my bed, alone in the night. That is when I must remember to invite myself—and to accept that invitation fully.

I'd like to return to the wisdom I learned from the Quakers. To use Martin Buber's language, there is a "clearly identifiable center" in the Quaker meeting, wherein everyone knows they come to sit and listen to the sacred. How they listen to the sacred and what they hear can be different for everyone. But the rules are: come in, be spacious, and stay open to the voice or voices of the sacred.

We all stand at the gateway of liminal time. As with the Quaker meeting, if we have a sense of deep knowing and hear such clarity of the sacred that it moves us to share, it's not ego-sharing. This is not the individualized persona sharing; it is the deepest sharing that only comes out of union, which brings us back to surrender. This is connection.

Quakers come into a meeting with no need or agenda to say anything, but there is a common language, meaning, and purpose. Similarly, to be receptive, there needs to be agreement that we are here together, bringing our essence into a place where we have created some sense of safety, so that when we feel those tender moments, we can breathe and say, "This is good. I can explore even what challenges me. I'm willing to go down the rabbit hole where sometimes it's dark and sometimes I'm scared out of my wits. And I'm also available to surrender to the *other*, to the majesty of the sacred moment, taking breathers into the softness as I go along."

Again, that may sound like a review, but what comes next is the life we live *beyond* the rabbit hole. In Hollywood terms, maybe you view that quality of receptivity as a bit of a sequel to the previous qualities we've covered, and I hope you can see where the story takes us next.

We must fearlessly confront the initial discomfort of the change our growth—and subsequent joy—demand. We must soften ourselves, and keep softening ourselves. We must love ourselves deeper and deeper, continuing to be ever more receptive to these tender moments and understandings. In this softening, there is not judgment but choice. In that choice, there is the possibility of growth. Would we rather be in a place of gentle loving-kindness toward ourselves so that we can be receptive to the other, or do we continue to sit through reruns of our lives' melodrama, remaining in the ever-increasing cycles of the same storylines that hold us in bondage?

Let's look at another real-world example. In my current consulting work in rural Idaho, where I look at wellness in education, I've watched uniting and wholeness enter a school district in remarkable ways as a direct result of that reprioritization. One man I've worked with is Jay, the previous superintendent of one of the districts.

Three and a half years ago, when we first met and I explained the possibilities I envisioned for creating an environment of well-being for employees, Jay told me, "I think you're full of shit." I realized I like this guy. The asshole in me could see the asshole in him. That's like "Namaste" in New York. Jay had a familiar narrative that he clung to, but the problem with familiar narratives is that they seldom lead us to new results.

Because of our mutual receptivity, our ability to identify ourselves and our spark in one another, Jay and I were able to move past the triviality of our disagreements to get into alignment. Because of our mutual receptivity, we were able to move into a relationship of trust and respect, in which we both knew we were going to do what we said we were going to do and do it honorably. This led Jay to take a major risk and introduce me to the current superintendent, which led to the recent kick-off of a new approach to well-being for the school district. That included bringing acupuncturists, naturopaths, and body workers into a new environment, where three hundred employees participated in breakout sessions and opened themselves to new possibilities for their health care and realignment in an incredibly stressful, impacting field.

On my last visit, I had dinner with Jay and his wife and found myself so touched by his openness to what I have to offer. Now he and I can sit and have the most elegant and caring conversations, even while we disagree. Our conversations are so respectful that when we finish them, we literally embrace one another.

To move to a place of living in love and healing, geologist-turned-philosopher Greg Braden asks: Do we love enough to go past polarity to a place "where all experience is viewed as creation knowing itself, experiencing the consequences of its own choice?"

This is the central question of our time. Are we willing to live in compassion in the midst of a world that lives in polarities? And are we willing to live within life's struggle and ambiguity, exploring the gradations of life, rather than retreat to simple linear answers? Healing lies in meeting the wonder and the unknowing, yet staying open to the miraculous. As such, the real question remains: what are we willing to change in our own lives to accomplish that shift and empower ourselves to grow?

Braden wrote that through shifting our feelings, we shift the way we see the world around us. In other words, if we want to embrace a life of light, *we can choose to see light.* By staying open to the possibility of dark entering in, we can offer it compassion, rather than a cure or a fight. It is this surrender that brings in the light once again, and in the light is always gratitude. This is a transcendent attempt at balance and self-love.

Once you have the basic material needs met in life, the further need to break off and conquer stems from internal imbalance. It also comes from the illusion of separation and false division. Hundreds of years ago, this aggression was a useful motivation, as humanity was in flux with its environment. We were in a time when many cultures were pilgrims of their humanity. The world has changed. Now the wilderness that requires courage to navigate exists within yourself.

And so here we are, once again pondering that elusive meaning of life. I can tell you this. If the only meaning of life were to win, we'd never need to leave the house. We could play video games all day long, and our new gods could be those fleet athletes whose names are printed upon on the jerseys we wear. These are distractions, meaningless accomplishments. If that was all we had to prioritize our needs and actions, our lives would be mirrors of the illusion of vicarious success, and what a waste that would be.

The ego works much the same as those instincts of the animal in the wild; it abhors vulnerability. At some point that was probably a survival instinct. But when does it become a liability? It will tell you lies about yourself so that you'll avoid reflection and won't see your own weakness. And so, what weakness is present is unresolved.

When confronted with higher, demanding truth, the ego builds a Maginot Line, just like the French battle tactic in WWII. They built the most elaborate trench system known to man. It had billets, supplies, even movie theaters. It was thought to be impregnable. There was only one problem. The cannons only pointed one way. The French were easily overrun when the enemy flanked them and poured in from the back. It's the same kind of flashy, but useless, front the ego puts up as defense. We no longer live life in the wild. But predators still seek us out. Your Stranger is your most valuable ally in fortifying your foundation to combat these threats and keep your head high. The time has come to meet your Stranger.

PRACTICE

I want you to court your Stranger.

Find the technique that feels the most natural to you; it could be writing, drawing, dancing, or even simply chatting to yourself. Do what you have chosen at the same time each day, three times a day (it doesn't have to be for a long time).

Keep at it! This creates discipline, strength, and knowing. Your Stranger will come to you, and after a while, what was once hard will become compulsive!

Discover yourself through a new story. This may feel uncomfortable for a while, even painful. Go in anyway. You've already known pain; it is what brought you here. Every step out you took toward imbalance, you must take to return to balance. Tiptoe if you need to, and stay until you walk in with heart and head erect. You are mighty! Have courage and smile.

BEING SUCCESS

So you are busy in the world,
Being success and looking strong,
But we know that inside,
You are a child
Looking for who you are—
Like the rest of us
Who cry or want to...
For the mother who loved too much
And the father who couldn't speak.
You want to know
Why you push so hard,
Why you sit with others,
Quoting the latest achievers
As they don't show their pain.
Take a chance;
Open to the other.
You may find
They bleed like you
And need to cry
The long, loud shriek
That hurts as it winds
Its way to your core.
Speak from where it's felt.
What can happen
Except hearing your truth
And knowing you belong?

AND SAY YES

You flitter through space
With beauty and ease,
Yet you're afraid to slow down
For fear of falling
Deeply.
Confronted with sight,
You might see the
Caring coming your way—
Not an ordinary caring, but
A missing piece
You have kept distant
And safe...
Or so you think.
So you fly even faster,
Keeping public attention
From private concern
And the stuff
Where the shadow resides.

But you could choose
To slow down just enough,
To allow for possibility,
And maybe wonder in awe
Of a life embraced.
The pain will still come
As the waves splash against the earth,
But just as they do,
They recede into time
To gather strength and insight
Before the next barrage.
Even nature can change course
And surrender as a power
To a new potent way,
Adding soft and vulnerable to control and knowing.
Once in a little while,
We allow for surprise;

We open to touch.
Once in a little while,
We allow a tear to warm
As it slides down our skin,
Opening portals of exuberant fear,
Making the wings too heavy to fly away.
Once in a little while,
We take a sacred chance
To come home
And say yes.

YES

Into the "yes"—
It feels strange,
As though I've been taken hostage
Into another land
With smiles and chatting
going on all around.
Where am I, and who asked for this?
It's hard for me to hide;
I always sit in the back…
This room is round.
I can't find a place to hide,
And others are looking at each other,
But no one's voice is dominating
or leading a way.
It feels spacious, unnerving.
How do I find a place
As no one pushes or tells,
Allowing for me to enter or not?
Someone has always been in front
Spouting stuff as right and wrong.
So often it's hard to find my way,
To listen in the quiet.
So where are the talkers—
those who tell
Which way it all goes?
As I hear quiet, the unnerving
Presence of "yes"
Enters as a whisper.
And without loud wind
Beating down my armor,
Its sound is stronger, spacious,
And I slowly feel me—
Sacred—
Joy.

MAKE ROOM

It's as though a door opened,
Taking us into another dimension
Where the gods
Actually offered a ride
Into our true nature,
And it is love:

The place where poets write
And mystics journey far.
But this time it's available
For our mortal lives,
As the touch of your true nature
Is greeted by sounds of joy
And felt as ecstasy
Both coursing in our bodies
And singing with the angels
In all the souls of heaven.

How rare to allow in union...
To laugh because we're tickled
By the cherubim as they play in our desire.
How rare to hear the sounds of dancing hearts
Because we said yes
To that sacred place
Where the gods even stand in awe
Of the human finding home.
Even the holy opens her doors
To invite the lovers in.

Make room at the table,
For the journey has been long
And the hunger great.
Make room so we can feed
Each other, and
Proclaim aloud to listen to our hearts
As though it always mattered
And our very life is real.

IN THE GARDEN

In the garden of my heart
Where the blooms come
Early in the year
And want to stay
To greet me with the colors
That warm and excite,
I know there is a season
For growth and one for rest.
But the beauty and smells
Of God
Can be with me
Throughout my life,
For the heart holds
Patterns of memory,
Circulating my being,
Sending impulses to the nerves
Of my soul.
And the colors of your passion
Comingle with the sweet spices
Of our love
So I can hold tender joy
As the buds explode
With their lush embrace.

THE GIFT

It's a gift
From the sacred
Mystery of life
How two souls
Can find one another,
Even in their fear
And self-imposed isolation,
For we guard against
Penetration
Of our private world,
Remaining in exile,
All safe and secure,
Or so we think—
We forget our heart
Has closed
As the price to pay,
And it's been so long
That the touch
Of the other
Is cause for alarm.

BRING IN THE SUN

God, claim me,
For alone
I just can't last,
And life with all
Its cruelty
Can be lovely as well.
I know now it's
In the choice.
Careful with grace,
I can make
It work.
Please fill me
With your warmth, for
Alone it is so cold
And dark.
Bring in the sun
So I can see and feel
Your loving embrace.
Together life is full
And the burdens
Shared.

WIDE OPEN

Oh, Love, how
You keep me warm,
Even with a heart
Wide open to the elements,
As though I'm naked
To the world.
I come to you
With nothing on.
I come because I'm called
To enter with the other
In your name,
Not mine.
As a messenger
Of the Divine,
I journey
Not for me alone.
There's only we
In the union
Of Blessed's embrace.

CHAPTER SEVEN

Befriending

And the day came when the risk to remain tight in a bud was more painful than the risk it took to blossom.

ANAÏS NIN

"HI, I'M YOUR STRANGER. WHO ARE YOU...?"

Hopefully, the *connection* that this journey is helping you make and the awareness of its gravity and significance is encouraging you to find a more intimate love for yourself. That is exactly where this journey is designed to lead you. Return to the truth that you are worth loving and *are* loved, deeply, by this world. Befriending our Stranger is the way we find our way home. In the last chapter, you learned to trust your Stranger. Now you must become the person your Stranger can trust. You must reestablish your intimacy with the divine, prioritizing harmony with your fellow humans, by living in honorable accordance with your highest self. You must learn to be free.

You are powerful. You are more powerful than you realize. Now this is where the tough love comes in—when you see what you must do to maintain that sincere self-love: Befriend your Stranger and act. Shed the mask and *be* the real you.

Don't be scared. At its core, befriending your Stranger is about both holding on and letting go. Letting go can be so challenging. Yet, as the changing seasons illustrate, trying to hold on to something that was really designed to be transitory creates imbalance. Your Stranger wants to see the real you. Release your self. Take off the mask. Together, what do you and your Stranger see now?

You started this journey because you wanted change, and that's where I've brought you. We have looked at reclaiming and proclaiming ourselves. We have learned to honor and discern the voice of divinity within ourselves and our neighbor. We befriend our Stranger when we act from an empowering softening of our hearts, and I have talked about ways to invite and encourage that softness and tenderness.

We find our most authentic motivations in liminal time, and then we strip ourselves down and change the way we live. This does influence the world. So many of us lower our personal standards and compromise values that really matter to us with the excuse, "That's just the way the world is." Stop saying that. The world is what we make it, we the collective. And as I have said, we are all connected, so every positive move you make in some way actively affects the whole and creates a better world.

Now we come to the point of action. That is when a philosophy becomes alive! That is where real healing takes place. The clearest way to honor the direction we are now called to is to seek out meaningful, productive union to accomplish these goals. I'm not asking you to change the world. I'm asking you to change *your* world, and act from a place reflecting the gravitas of that shift. On second thought, I *am* asking you to change the world.

We need to make the required changes to our activities, vices, imbalances, addictions, passions, relationships, and priorities to accommodate what has the deepest meaning for us. The difference between this and a religion is that I can't tell you what those things are, because they are different for everyone. Yet this is what I mean by befriending your Stranger: when you identify the deeper meanings and make those changes to accommodate them and open your heart, you reconnect to the person you are meant to be. You will see that you are now what you have been looking for the whole time.

Few Americans of this era understand the word *contentment*. Most of us have a mindset of scarcity, of not-enoughness. We try to fill the voids, which we perceive as empty space. This is a pointless process that leads to never-ending appetite, makes us see one another as rivals, and cultivates an urge to conquer, and then to define ourselves through the ego-based struggles of conquest. But if we're receptive to all of the diverse offerings available to us, and if we hold to the previous steps we have engaged, that mindset can shift. As the Sufi mystic poet Rumi suggests, beyond wrongdoing and right-doing, we can meet outside in a field of abundance, a mystic garden, so to speak.

More and more, we are pitched that same golden calf that the holy men and philosophers of the world have been warning us of for thousands of years. We could sit back and say, "That's just the way the world is," and invest in that golden bullshit, or we can rise to our best selves and collectively create a better world that suits the virtues and values that we know come from a deeper truth. We can demand more, starting with ourselves. But to do this, we need our claim on sanity, which comes from living authentically. Befriend and then become your Stranger. Live a life you are proud of. Start small. Make little, but meaningful shifts toward your values.

Currently, in the United States, we have elected officials who act as though democracy is about hoarding and not sharing. We have a president in the White House who threatens and bullies the world on a macro level and, on a micro level, insults and degrades any of the citizens he represents who question or threaten his idea of the monolith he is attempting to create. We have senators who have a lifetime of free health care but want to take it away from millions.

Thankfully, these officials are not the only examples we have of what the world can look like. We can look to Viktor Frankl, the author of *Man's Search for Meaning*, who found meaning while confined within a concentration camp. Like most of the victims of the Holocaust, he was displaced from his home by war and terror and the murderous policies of a genocidal madman. But he didn't lose himself to that depressing narrative. Instead he created logotherapy, a psychological model based on finding purpose and meaning in any situation.

We can look at another great spiritual exile, the monk Thich Nhat Hanh, who, in response to war in Vietnam, was exiled in France from his physical home and created Engaged Buddhism, knowing that no matter where he stood, he created his home and carried it with him.

We can look to the great leader Nelson Mandela, who spent twenty-seven years in an eight-foot-wide prison cell for his beliefs, yet in bondage found the fertile soil to continue cultivating himself, emerging to lead South Africa beyond the chains of apartheid and never succumbing to the chains of hating the people who put him there. Even in chains, Mandela stood taller than most men ever will.

In diaspora with thousands of his displaced people, the Dalai Lama finds himself at home around the world, carrying the seeds of his faith, Tibetan Buddhism, with him wherever he goes and planting them along the way to provide for those who follow.

All of these men live in a way that reflects a deep sense of union with the world and clearly demonstrates a spirit of awakened receptivity. They are able to listen and clearly discern, with truly open hearts. Even when confined or incarcerated, these men found a freedom within, based on hope and self-awareness, that eludes so many of us in much kinder circumstance. These men befriended and became their own Strangers, powerfully articulate against all their adversaries' deceptions and society's attempts to break their wills. They became lighthouses to a world that desperately needs more powerful, authentic human beings like them.

When life overwhelms me, I think of them, and many others, and I recall the truth that the journey of life is a carving tool designed to create the people we are meant to be. It is easy to distract ourselves from this truth for a while, but we will not know the peace of fulfillment until we embrace it. If you look at people like those I mentioned and find them to be heroic, or noble, then ask yourself, "What am I? What am I called to be from deep within in this real life that I'm living?"

You are not being called to become someone else. It's time to come clean with who you should have been the whole time and move forward into the real you, one sincere step at a time.

Years ago, I was a practitioner of acupuncture, but now my primary experience of acupuncture is receiving it. Megan, the practitioner I've seen for the last seven years, is both my naturopath and acupuncturist, but I call her my angelic healer. At our last appointment, I came in anxious, clutching a bunch of papers. My gut felt twisted and tight. I'd just received lab results about recent blood work and had gotten lost in research about statins and Chinese herbs, whatever I could do to deal with what my Western medical doctor had characterized as high cholesterol. When I got to Megan's office, I was nervously remembering cancer. My heart was skittering. I handed her the lab results and continued to blabber about the research I'd done, holding fast to the belief that I had a big problem and had to do something about it.

She told me to stop talking and held up the results. "The ratio of LDL and HDL is perfect," she said. "What's the problem?"

Where the other doctor saw a need for statins, Megan saw the possibility that my body was already taking care of itself, as well as other ways to decrease cholesterol. As I experienced Megan's receptivity, I noticed myself soften, too.

With that softness, Megan led me out of my head, which was racing with cholesterol research, and into my heart and body, which craved spaciousness and healing. We talked about my sleep and the sensations in my legs, and soon she had me up on the table with about thirty needles in my feet and elsewhere.

"Are you going to stop anytime soon?" I asked, joking. "I can't even move a limb."

"That's all right," she said. "You're going to lie here and rest."

So, I did, noticing my abdominal cavity expanding, my gut relaxing. I found myself smiling.

This kind of permission to surrender, to shift out of fear, is also a gift we can offer ourselves. Take a moment right now to experience something, someone, or some idea very different from your own and notice where you experience tightness. Then send a soft, healing breath into that place and keep sending it until the tightness subsides.

Are we available to soften ourselves, and to be there with *surrender* (a challenging word)? We have reached the tough love section of this journey, and with it comes a new question: what are you willing to DO to achieve it? Ultimately, if you thought philosophizing was in and of itself your solution, you would be content with the same trap of vicarious pseudo-reality so many of us are conditioned to live within. Presuming you chose to do the self-work to facilitate change in your life, now it is time to DO.

We have tilled the soil, so to speak, with philosophy, prayer, meditation, self-awareness, and seeking to make the connections between us more tangible. These are all crucial steps toward a more authentic, rewarding life. Now we must follow that with the harder part: changing our lives by DOING. We've talked about our actions and teamwork in a broad, vocational sense. Now, let's talk about what gets you out of bed in the morning.

In the last chapter, we looked at how imbalance and anxiety, depression and fear are all forms of addiction to a world that feels unnatural. What are you willing to actively change in your own life to reconnect with yourself and the world and see them both as beautiful parts of a sacred whole?

I'll say this directly. Of all the messages I hear so often, one of the most misguided is "I don't have time." The reality is that each and all of us, from the laziest person you know to the saints, holy men, beggars, and kings of this world, all have one thing in common: our day has twenty-four hours.

That's the time we have. Every day, the "difference" we make, through living authentically, *as ourselves*, is in how we prioritize our actions during that time, how we view our resources and gifts, and how much responsibility we take in honoring our fleeting time on earth.

If you are struggling with this, just reflect on the opposite of rigidity, consumerism, dogma: the idea of spaciousness, the idea of freedom, the idea of love. Sit with it for a few moments. Which *really* feels more real after even just a few minutes of quiet breathing? When you unplug and disconnect from society's signal, even for a few heartbeats, you'll find your Stranger begging to enter your life.

Now decide which you would prefer in your life. It is *your* choice. Learn to take responsibility for your choice. Yes, we are all connected, and yes, there is a system in place designed to inflate ideals of individuality while oppressing the notion of autonomy. So, rejoice in your choice and your opportunity to re-create your paradigm as a receptive, authentic being. We have, at every moment, the precious gift of choice to stay in a place of soft, heart-centered welcoming.

We must also remember that *receptivity* and *surrender* do not mean giving away, caving in, or losing our sense of self. Instead, in softness and openness we are fully present, aware of the shadow side, even as we are letting in light.

Let me share with you a story of an incredibly balanced man I met, and how he spoke to something in me. A few years ago, I was working to set up a division with my company, Sophus, to facilitate healing retreats. I put a notice up on LinkedIn, asking for people who want to teach. Among the twenty responses was Tom's. After I narrowed the group down to the ten I would like to meet, Tom quickly rose to the top. All ten were good people, but with Tom, I had a totally different meeting.

If I recall, we met in Gig Harbor, Washington, at a wine bar that looked out over the water. What I remember clearly is that Tom instantly felt like a brother. With most new relationships, there's a dance of definitions—this is who I'll be, this is who you'll be. Not with Tom. For both of us, it was one of those rare spirit meetings, as though we'd known each other for years and lifetimes.

Tom had written a book called *Crazy Wisdom*, which was jovial and warm and playful. He was an economist who felt he knew little about money and a retired minister who questioned his belief. What Tom did know was receptivity and how to be in relationships with others, and how to live in a consistent manner that had deep meaning for him—and, through him, for others.

As we planned workshops and built a friendship, I moved to Gig Harbor from Portland, knowing I needed some space from Portland and not sure where to head next. A temporary move close to my new friend felt right. I made many a visit to Tom and Pam's house. We'd sit on the porch sometimes and share evening meals, and as happens with friends who are like family, when the conversation waxed long and the bottle of wine went empty, I'd spend the night in their guest room, happy to share tea and more good conversation and laughter in the morning.

Our time together felt light and easy. Although Tom was willing to be playful, he never had to play any role or expected me to play one either. It was a refreshing distinction. We waste so much of the precious time we have trying to convince ourselves and others of the masks our ego convinces us to wear.

Tom wanted to do a workshop on the "stranger" spirit of money, to explore how many of us lack a clear or peaceful relationship with money. I liked the idea and was already considering ways to incorporate some things from the spiritual autobiography work I'd done with other groups.

It seemed like a dream union. But, as it does, life pulled on the rug we sat upon. One day, Tom said he didn't feel well. Soon we discovered Tom had pancreatic cancer, news that was all too familiar to me.

What Tom needed was space to be with his family and deal with this news. With sadness at the sudden illness of my friend and unsure where to be, I told Tom I'd keep working on our ideas as I traveled to San Miguel de Allende, Mexico, where I'd considered moving. While I was there, Tom called, asking what I'd done on the description for our workshop.

"Hold your horses," I joked. "I'm going to have some mezcal, and we'll talk when I come back."

We never talked about the workshop again. By the time I returned to Gig Harbor, Tom had lost at least twenty pounds. My heart broke seeing my friend like this. Visiting with him on his porch, I struggled to hold it together.

"I don't have a future," Tom said, "so tell me something good."

I lost it, weeping in this tender shared place of heart. Even in this moment, we welcomed each other. No roles. No play-acting. Simply receptive and present.

Less than two months from his diagnosis, my friend, this vital being of love, was felled by a relentless cancer that gave no time for reflective healing. My time with Tom was rare and precious. Still, three years later, Tom is with me, as is the softness of heart he brought to our far too brief friendship.

As I said, "I don't have time" is one of the beliefs most toxic to love. We commodify one another by focusing on deadlines, fiscal agendas, and our coping mechanisms. Don't be ships passing in the night, failing to acknowledge gifts of love, refusing to listen to voices that have something important to say to you, pretending you have something better to do than to explore the world and learn as much as you can about it.

The time I spent with Tom was transformative and validating in a way that focusing solely on my business needs never could have been. Ultimately, what we make time for in our twenty-four-hour days, and what we make space for in our hearts, is what defines us. We have to keep our hearts soft, my friends, to reshape our lives to align with what is truly important. Softness, however, shouldn't be confused with weakness. Where would I be if, when I was diagnosed with cancer, the people close to me decided I was no longer an "asset," or that keeping my company was no longer practical?

Befriending your Stranger is a place of power, but this is very different from the false understanding of power that has to be over something or someone. Some of the worst misinterpretations of scripture use the words "having dominion over" when the *real* meaning of power is "having partnership with." Knowing the root of your needs and pursuing them honestly, rather than falling into toxic cycles, requires time and a deep appraisal of your motivations and agendas to see how they line up with the values that call to you. What you're doing is training yourself to listen to your heart.

The connection of this paradigm shift between knowing and feeling, between mind and heart, is essential here, and something that's been beautifully researched by the HeartMath Institute. HeartMath research has been scientifically documenting and verifying what mystics have been saying for thousands of years before Western science even existed: that the *heart* is the core of our being and the center of the system that sends impulses to the brain. Accordingly, the brain sends out neurotransmitters to the rest of the body, which has a physiological response so that it's in resonance with the *heart*. With practice, we can cultivate this resonance that allows us, gives us permission, to really come to ourselves and others through that place of softness.

I was raised in a home that certainly cherished loving each other. Our family was the center of my parents' lives. Along with that, I was raised with the sad understanding that love came with control, manipulation, and both having and asserting power. As long as we children were doing things to please the parents, love was liberally bestowed. Conversely, in the face of displeasure, affection was rationed as though it were in short supply. My sister and I learned to survive through the pretense of pleasing. In my case, that led to being "the good boy." Because I was always trying to please, I stayed out of touch with myself and my true sense of power.

This was not receptivity. This behavior came from a place where the halls and corridors of the heart are narrow and cold. It's difficult to be *receptive* when always calculating how to take care of the other so I receive the least amount of pain. At sixty-eight years of age, I find this conditioned dynamic still occurs, but I've trained myself to recognize and shift it.

After the divorce, in the fall of 2015, I went to San Miguel de Allende, a place I hadn't been to with my second wife. I wanted a place just for me, and my friends said it was a fun area. It felt like a fresh start. It was certainly better than doing nothing and succumbing to grief. And it was a good move. This is what I mean by being proactive. The move to Mexico gave me some of my life back, and my days were filled with walking, playing, searching, and listening.

My favorite place was Parque Juarez, the most beautiful park in town. I felt at home with myself there. Right on the park was Hotel Antigua Santa Monica, a little hotel built as a ranchero. On Sundays they did the most wonderful brunch, and I always got the same thing, which tasted to me just like potato latkes—a flavor of home. Surrounded by greenery, beautiful architecture, and roaming peacocks, I loved to sit there and be quiet.

In that quiet, I started becoming more aware of messages coming from within, messages both large and small. I didn't question their veracity; I sat with them. Living in San Miguel, I realized I was done with cars and built my life around being able to walk where I needed. And as I made space for hope and transformation, the urge to return to writing arose. I decided to come back to this book, the one you're reading right now, and I decided I would finish it. This was a major leap of faith—to write my heart and invite a transformative experience into my life.

I made the leap, because in coming to San Miguel, I had come back to center, that place where the quiet truth is, where the love is, where joy and passion flourish. Listening brought me beyond the darkness and back home—back to that place of alignment, the one I don't have to travel to get to. But I did have to seek it out. Listening is not passive; it is receptive. I hope I am helping you understand this distinction.

It should be part of your covenant to act on the signs you are sent. Often these signs seem to speak to a larger version of ourselves than we are aware of. So we temper our listening with hope. Hope sends the beauty of Aha! impulses through my being and allows me to say a big yes to union—with my truest self, with the Divine, with all beings. I now live in my Stranger's reality, a little more free in this world than I would have been.

When I discuss these matters with people who are struggling, I almost always get the same responses: I don't have enough time to listen or meditate. I need a quick answer. I want my life to change without changing anything in it. I want to learn what I don't know without actually altering my perspective based on the new information. I want to continue to hold on to my habits/lifestyle/views, regardless of consequence.

That sounds a lot like addiction to me. And I always say the same thing in response: You are living your life. Your greatest responsibility, beyond anything else, is to live your life authentically. If pursuit of external things and standards you had no hand in creating for yourself is causing you to live dismissively, or to run yourself into the ground trying to please others, or to hate living, you are not prioritizing properly. Success, or rather, the illusion of material success, is of no significance or value if you are not present in your own life and are disconnected from your own divinity, family, and self. We all get one life. That life is the greatest gift and asset you have, and honoring that is your responsibility.

Is that some hippie talk? It isn't. Anybody who tries to convince you otherwise is manipulating you. Ask your elders, those closest to the veil, what they would have done differently. You might be surprised by their answers. Which is not to say that befriending your

Stranger is mutually exclusive to success—many of the MOST successful people are those with the clearest direction and the deepest harmony within themselves.

As I understand it, when we truly put out into the universe that we are in partnership with the Divine and we ask for support, guidance, and assistance, we receive it. But change cannot begin with an existential *Waiting for Godot* mindset. You must get up in the morning, go out the door, and get on with things. If you see life as a burden, don't expect blessing to meet ingratitude. Meet the world beyond your mind. When we are befriending our Stranger, we are actively finding balance and then acting. When you receive the deepest answers that compel you to connect and move forward in your life, rather than retreat or avoid it, you start to rise into your own existence.

PRACTICE

Now let's expound on the practice we began at the end of the last chapter, "Meeting," to help you court and respond to liminal time so you can befriend your Stranger. You'll be glad that you did.

If you haven't done so already, take the time to set up your practice area in a comfortable way. Create a place where you don't feel stressed, overwhelmed, or distracted by anything other than the present. Exercise living in no time; create an altar in your home that you pass every day and begin to sit there, no phones, just you and your thoughts. Watch them, listen to them, with no judgment or need to do anything. Make space to walk, walk, walk.

Ask yourself: Where does this connection lead me? What does my Stranger want of me? What can I do to live more authentically?

This is the most important aspect of healing. We want to belong, sometimes so much that we surrender ourselves. Befriend your Stranger. Belong to yourself again.

DETOUR

It had to be self-loathing
That brought me to you.
"I never saw a man change and grow
So fast into one who
Is intentional about his life."
Yet love was not enough, throwing the tickets
In my face on your birthday eve,
Or moving to a land down under
As the work of a life was valued less than.

"They don't live with you,"
I heard,
Coming at times when control
No longer worked.
I believed
I was fucked up on the inside
And I did deserve to be rolled up, laying
In the grass with riveting pain
Without a budge of care.
I caused the breakdown of society
Ending our financial system by not hiding the gold carefully—
It needs to be moved each day.

Using the power of physical sensation
And manipulation of a man working
On growth and gentle love,
Bringing self fully
With wounded heart into the battlefields of care.
Strip me down, taking all my clothes,
Hiding them so I had to stay;
Using a boy child as
Insurance for a time planned well in advance.
How to maintain sensitive self
To come wide open, fully engaged—
Sensitive, strong power of inner wisdoms?

Controlling tender minds and hearts
Is the violence of the ages:
It speaks about illness,
Bringing teaching and guidance,
When really taking over
Hurting with stories of love and care.
But it was Monopoly, and I was trying Life.
Self-loathing, little compassion;
Questioning in the pockets where the lost keys
Went since swimming in the womb.
We're all living in tender places
So much that we keep busy,
Running rather than stopping for dynamic rest or
Reflective moments to catch ourselves;
Looking to love as a home
Where holding is unquestioned and present.
This home is screaming through our land
For touch with gentle caress,
Bringing in our wounded words,
Helping us open to our fears in this
Together, knowing the Holy is bleeding for
Our world.

Egos getting us through our days, not the toys
Of lost adults' cleverly learned manipulations
Controlling within this fragile place.
Hold the circle of wisdom, bringing sacred where we
Journey together, no excuse to hurt
With intention.
Be God's image;
Be us;
Be.

WHERE IS HOME

After the hurt split your heart,
You don't want to listen.
But you know it's knocking harder
Each day as you run the other way.

Body in motion, breaking apart
As one side wants to find its way back
While the other still claims it's too soon.
And you don't know yet which one sings
Into your soul; is that true,
Or is the clarity leading you to die?

Death into new birth, not bad—
Go now into the hurt where your juice
Is running amok as it finds its own ground.
You want love so bad you shut it out,
Telling yourself stories of the illusion
Of your life,
Or stories of the others
Finding it less painful...so you tell yourself.
It's also not alive.
Go in; it may hurt some more
Toward the hurt.
Claim your place
And come to your home.

I was beginning to trust
And shift from being the giver
To the sharer.
Too many years believing I had to be all;
Never learned boundaries
Nor taking care of self, bringing my fullness,
Sharing in togetherness,
Shaping a life each strong and each together.

Fragile, coming with ghosts,
With stories,
Ancestors refusing to leave.
Supporting each other to be with
In the Thou, present within the now.

Beginning to open to new creation;
Ghosts moving on, replaced with touch and play—
Sometimes hard, staying with.
In the no, I was saying yes.
Even in the not knowing, embracing wonder
With some trepidation, each day awake to surprise.
And when "Run" enters thought,
We come together, growing into Thou.

CHAPTER EIGHT

Appreciating

Because of your smile, you make life more beautiful. Fear keeps us focused on the past or worried about the future. Every breath we take, every step we make, can be filled with peace, joy, and serenity.

THICH NHAT HANH

GRATITUDE

In gratitude
I come
For the guidance
I receive
During moments of fear,
Knowing that I need
Only listen
For the way
Back to wholeness.
Thank You.
Amen.

WE NEED TO GIVE THANKS JUST FOR THE SHEER DELIGHT OF BEING given this gift of life. We've shared so many moments of recreation. We've taken an incredible journey together. But we must remain present in our objectives. Entitlement and avarice poison our ability to be present and to passionately resonate with the blessings of life. These toxic mentalities throw us into imbalance again and again. Now we will take time to learn how to use the tools we have been practicing to restore balance through consciously cultivating gratitude and redeveloping a healthy, natural paradigm.

Rabbi Heschel said, "To pray is to take notice of the wonder, to regain a sense of the mystery that animates all beings, the divine margin in all attainments. Prayer is our humble answer to the inconceivable surprise of living." For Heschel, who saw the holy in everything, prayer was a way to thank the source for the gift. He wrote, "It is gratefulness which makes the soul great." Such gratitude opens our hearts, allows them to love and also to heal. If we want to heal, it's time to bring the sacred into every corner by honoring and blessing the movements of everyday life.

Again, I often find profundity in returning to the mentality I was blessed with as a child. When I was an intern minister at the Unitarian Church in Virginia, I so enjoyed being with the youth. Once, I prepared a special program for the primary school children. Parents brought their children to me for the liberal, inclusive religious education that Unitarians did well. I wanted to lead them in a mettā, or loving-kindness, meditation and wondered how I might do this in a way that would work for them. I had an idea. At the local plant nursery, I purchased landscape rocks, and on Sunday morning, I handed one to each child in the classroom.

As the children played with the rocks, I asked them to close their eyes and say aloud, "May my mom feel good," and then "May my dad feel good," and as they continued to feel the rocks, move on to bless teachers, friends, and so on. At first, there was giggling and some silly comments, but after a bit the atmosphere shifted into gentle quiet with a profound sense of care. The kids were in the zone.

I also noticed a lovely shift of awareness in the foyer by the classroom, where the parents observed their children. After this meditation time, a number of things happened. The kids said thank you, and the parents did as well.

Seven or eight parents even asked me, "When can we do this too?" They were very curious about it and about finding other ways to shift their focus.

That's an interesting question, "When can we do this too?" What was stopping them? The parents were mostly professionals, many with high-level careers, but they rarely gave themselves time to meditate on the blessings in their lives. They'd brought their children to me for intellectual stimulation, and yet watching their children have a Sabbath, they realized they were missing out on this gift.

The whole experience felt to me like a gratitude- and love-fest, from the meditation with the children to the conversations afterward. Healing is about this kind of loving-kindness—opening our hearts, being gentle, whole, and related. Healing thus comes through continuous relatedness and the persistent destruction of artificial walls of separation. That Sunday morning, we went from having an inside of the classroom and an outside of the classroom to all of us being in one grateful space together.

Years ago, I spent a weekend in bed reading Heschel's final book, *A Passion for Truth*. At the time, the brightest part of my life was studying at the Graduate Theological Union in Berkeley. Otherwise, my weekdays were taxing, to say the least, driving an hour and a half to get to work and sell cars, then driving home to collapse. I was also still receiving treatments for Hodgkin's, so on days I had chemo, I'd go to Stanford, get zapped, and then travel to work or home or school. I kept a container in the car in case the nausea came. It was a time when it would have been easy to get discouraged.

The weekend I brought Heschel's book to our house in Petaluma, I barely got out of bed. My heart was in a wounded openness, tender and raw, and I couldn't put the book down. Heschel goes into depth about the incomprehensible idea that we were created in the image of God, just to be eternally grateful and a blessing to each other.

His words touched me profoundly. To me, Heschel was Jewish in a universal way; his language was familiar for me, as was his role as the prophetic voice—one screaming in the wilderness, one that has to tell and live in truth. When he was asked about Judaism and religion, Heschel emphasized that Sabbath didn't take place in a grand cathedral but was really about understanding time and learning how to live inside its true value. For him, the Sabbath is when we move from the profane, worldly material-based rest of the week to a time of gratefully paying attention to the sacredness of life.

I felt such resonance with all he shared. In my tender state, I could hear him. I basically cried all weekend—wounded, open, and grateful for the blessing of being a part of this rat race we call life. I say "rat race" in partial jest. There might be some justification for a belief in that manufactured reality, but if we step back to witness it and be grateful, we can come to perceive life as so much more—and don't you long for that?

In America, we embrace irony. We set aside time to celebrate the joy of all the blessings we have once a year during Thanksgiving. Most of the Bibles and holy books that inform the American culture suggest celebrating a form of Sabbath once a week, but holy capitalism stomped that out as being unprofitable. So now we do it once a year, and even declare it a national holiday. We gather our family together and "relax" on Thanksgiving.

But rather than prayer, "Thanksgiving" is filled with noise, in the form of parades, sports, and almost insurmountable goals of hospitality. Yet we do, ideally, take some degree of time to rest and respond to our families and the many good hands we have been dealt. We breathe easy, and we take naps. Then what happens? By the next morning, Christmas songs are blaring from the radio and we are flooding the streets, beating each other up to get ten dollars off the price of a printer. It's almost as though, in a society of pure capitalism, even the peace of mind of a deep breath must immediately be stomped out and reversed completely. And this is no accident. Corporations must double down in fueling that endless consumer hunger, lest you wake up and they lose their hold on you. Again, we might take that for granted as "just the way things are," but in reality, it's a new and evolving trend in our culture.

What are *you* getting out of it?

If your answer is "very little," let's look at ways to reignite and embolden a transcendent spirit of gratitude to add dimension to the significance of your life. The Quakers say that because the light is within us all, we have to treat each other with complete and grateful attention, knowing that we are each a piece of that sacred Divine.

Given the trajectory of my life, I often find the medical field is ripe with examples illustrating these points. While treating each other with gratitude is essential to healing, not everyone in the medical profession understands this necessity. In the past, the absence of gratitude has led to disconnection and hurdles in my lengthy path to recovery. Fortunately, I was blessed to receive care from one who did live in the gratitude dynamic at a time when I needed it most.

Michael, a Jewish man who went to a Quaker college, traveled to China to study Chinese medicine in the original language. When he returned to the United States, he opened a prestigious clinic just outside of San Francisco. I met this brilliant physician when he got involved with the naturopathic school I'd started. When I was diagnosed with Hodgkin's, I'd already known him for almost two years and went to him for additional treatment.

When he took my pulse, sometimes he would spend twenty minutes or a half hour writing prolific longhand notes in Chinese. I was amazed at his ability to notice something happening in my body and tune in to the particular history related to it. One time, he felt my pulse, paused, and wrote. Then he said, "What was it that happened when you were two years old, and you hurt something?"

Surprised at the specificity, I asked, "What the hell, Michael?"

He simply repeated the question.

"Oh, yeah," I said, remembering, astonished. "I was jumping on my father and bumped my head on the radiator."

Reading the pulse was Michael's way of going into something beyond, to tap into a deep well of healing wisdom. And his perception enabled the connection we shared to have a huge impact on my healing process. Often I find modern medicine to be very reactionary—that is, it often seems to create a cycle of symptom treatment, which may fuel other maladies, instead of looking at deeper causes and healing them by a restoration of harmony. Sometimes, when Michael had an insight or thought during a session, he'd say, "I need to sit with this [new information]. I'll send you a letter in a few days."

Sure enough, a few days later, I'd receive a comprehensive letter, the likes of which I'd never seen. I deeply valued his skill at blending Chinese and Western medicine, drawing on his knowledge and resources and intuition, and coming up with treatment plans. With confidence, he'd tell me things like, "Okay Arnie, we're going to do this particular chemo protocol along with our treatments here. I checked in with the Italian doctor who specializes in this, and this is the one that works."

Unlike other medical professionals, who rushed in and out of appointments with me, Michael took his time and treated me with that complete grateful attention, sometimes spending an hour or two with me, as needed. When I met with other doctors who suggested other treatments, I always would say, "Before we do this treatment, I have to talk to Michael to confirm it's the best way to go." Eventually, they also valued what he had to offer, and he became a cancer consultant for Stanford.

If it weren't for Michael and his skill and compassion, I wouldn't be here. I was so grateful to him. So, what does this have to do with cultivating gratitude? The answer is SO MUCH! People look at appreciation as an A-to-B Pavlovian dynamic: I ring a bell, I get the cheese. Now that I have the cheese, I am grateful. Whatever, I showed up, I deserved it. This is how we think. In reality, the most significant aspect of gratitude is perception. When we have an unbalanced perspective, it is very hard to experience true gratitude, for several reasons.

For most life-forms on earth, the basic foundation for their "meaning" in life is to guarantee survival. That's their chief priority. Consciously or not, all life-forms cultivate survival through action and balance. As products of an *interdependent* ecosystem, though conflict exists, you rarely see exhibitions of addiction and emotional imbalance such as gluttony or depression. Humans and animals alike start with a base of childhood, where we are provided for as we grow and learn to connect to our environments to provide for ourselves. Balance is created through the cultivation of aggression and cooperation, instinct and learning, to remain a part of the cycle(s) of life.

In our own culture, the natural growth arc has been replaced by reliance on technology and a fabricated sense of entitlement. We remain children, expecting to be provided for because we feel entitled. This forms our base of perception. Everything beyond it is greed and gluttony. Then we add technologies through which we live vicariously. What at one point were tools that were designed to aid our lives have become our actual priorities. With that shift in priority has come isolation from one another and our surroundings. Instead of growing our own food, cooking it, and sharing meals together, we order fast food with an app and then consume it thoughtlessly, perhaps while looking at a screen. Instead of learning how to sew, how to make furniture, how to talk to the Divine through our own offerings of art and poetry, we order whatever we want online and it arrives in a day or two.

So, where effort and balance were once required to give meaning to life, a hole formed. We lost the desire to coexist, or be in harmony with our environments. Now we yearn to dominate, control, and conquer. The instincts we naturally have to thrive in abundance in our ecosystems have bled into our egos and mutated into something thoroughly unnatural. Corporate interests have seized upon this to create the culture of the consumer, replacing basic, natural hungers with constant, dizzying anxiety. No peace exists in appetites that can never be truly fulfilled. Watch the news. Some of the most unhappy, self-destructive people in our culture are actually those who have the most—who have bought into the lie with the most devotion. But where is their reward? Where is their peace?

When I look for the basic, foundational message of all the spiritual teachers and every spiritual teaching I've received during my quest to combat the toxic reprogramming of modern life, the antidote always seems to come down to gratefulness and compassion. When the Dalai Lama was asked to distill Buddhism down to one word, he said, "It's just compassion." Compassion for all aspects of being human; compassion because all life is interconnected. Rather than viewing life as a "race" in which the goal is to conquer, we should be viewing life as a journey in which we are all trying to survive together. And, with compassion, we can help one another thrive.

Ask yourself some questions. What are your key motivations in life... not philosophically, but practically: What gets you out of bed? What are things you feel you "deserve" in life, and why do you feel that way? Questioning helps us evaluate our foundations. We evaluate what we have, and we take what we want, and then we look for discrepancies in how we perceive them. We have looked at *redefining* ourselves and *reconnecting* with others; now let's figure out how we can *recondition* the stimuli we're bombarded with and create harmony between our desires, our blessings, and our responsibilities.

Has my life been easy? I've tried pretty hard to show you the ways in which it hasn't been. But there's no coherent reason to believe that life was ever meant to be "easy." That's a commercial for life. And believing it's the whole picture, or that a "whole" picture even exists, is one of the traps of entitlement and lazy living. I try not to fall into that trap, and so should you. Take that belief away from your foundation. Then strip yourself of the delusion that the sole meaning of life is to be the Western world's version of "happy," which really just means constantly stimulated appetites and ego gratification. There's no gravitas in that perspective. It's lazy, and it's no excuse for a life. Remove these toxic beliefs and your whole foundation will immediately shift.

I can say that my life has not been easy, but I know it is a gift, and it's up to me whether I choose to be receptive and open or trapped and miserable. My life has been an adventure. It remains a blessing. Each experience carves and crafts and hones me. I am grateful for every moment—the good, bad, and ugly—because each moment holds equal value—the gift of being.

I'm so grateful for masters like the Dalai Lama and Thich Nhat Hanh, for Buber and Heschel, for those many beings who have touched me and brought me back to that gratitude. I'm so grateful for the people I've invited into my life, the healers and friends who share their light with me. And I'm grateful to you, the reader, for giving me this chance to be in an I-Thou relationship with you. I'm not racing against you to get something and keep it for myself. We are in this journey together, and that is a magical, meaningful thing.

Indeed, on the surface, appreciation and gratefulness seem like simple ideas, yet they appear to be one of our larger challenges, particularly in today's environment which feeds control and gluttony. Appreciation is expansive and cannot exist in under the tight illusion of control. When I look at the dominant religious paradigm today in Western culture and the United States in particular, I see that we believe that everybody has to live according to particular precepts. We believe that this is living in accordance with God's rules. But I don't feel much gratefulness in such a belief system, one that leaves no room for questioning. And when I look at the world we have been given, I see evidence of an entirely different set of rules exhibited uniformly by the rest of creation—namely, balance and harmony.

How do we reawaken our passion for the unknown, the mystery, this journey of exploration to restore balance and harmony? First, we grow in awareness. In the United States and other parts of the world, we're allowing fascism to shut down our hearts, declaring that the heart isn't a good enough guide. But we have befriended our Stranger, so we know that's not true. We're being told to ignore the deep well of wonder and magic and instead drink from the poison well of addiction and false values. But we have reconnected to divinity and the font of creation.

Modern society is at the top of a food chain, destroying countless lives and families across the globe for the mere augmentation of our personal convenience. But we can help society move beyond the toxicity of our own making. The need for power and control comes from our deepest wounds. Those same instincts are what prevent those wounds from ever healing. No wonder so many of us can't sleep at night and anti-anxiety pills and opioid addictions are in full bloom in America. We've created an ecosystem and mindset not exhibited anywhere or by anything else in the natural world.

How do we step out of this toxic mentality? How do we find that expansive place where we remember that life is about sharing? How do we return to a place of appreciation and gratitude? I don't have purely philosophical answers for these questions. For me, the answers often come when I visit Portugal.

I'd heard about the magical place that is Portugal for a number of years, and I decided to give myself the gift of that healing journey. Landing very early on a morning in October, I took the subway to somewhere I didn't know and walked through neighborhoods in the largest city, Lisbon, looking for the room I had booked. Being raised in New York City, I had learned to be on guard every moment, even at 5 a.m., and yet, walking here in Lisbon, I felt strangely at peace. The sense of belonging, though I was in a country with a different language and culture, stays with me so powerfully that I return there whenever I can.

In describing Portugal, I have to use the word *magic*, but the magic is as real as the land, the sea, and the sky. The people exude a welcoming warmth I've rarely felt. Seeing people of various shades, colors, and persuasions holding hands, laughing, and making out on park benches never fails to waken an infectious spirit of joy in me. As I walk through this city of stunning architecture and parks, dazzling sky and water, a mellow well-being spreads through me, quite different from the intoxication or numbness of alcohol or drugs.

One early evening, I took a taxi, as my destination was a bit too far to get to on foot. I was going to Belém for a concert of fado, an eclectic music style seen as the soul of Portugal. I asked the driver if he'd lived in Lisbon for long, and he said yes, for most of his life, and that he loved living there. I asked why.

He said one word. "Tranquility."

Tranquility. His answer surprised me, as Lisbon is the largest city in the country. But he had found tranquility despite the hustle and bustle. When was the last time you felt tranquil while in a massive community? In fact, haven't we trained ourselves to generally find tranquility by running away from other people? Why is that? I liked his answer. And I had also experienced tranquility while there.

Can we claim that any large US city is tranquil? If not, then maybe we should shift our perception from feeling that "people" are the inherent barrier to our tranquility to seeing that "culture" is the barrier, and that luckily for us, culture is malleable. We can look at what we internalize and what we choose to contribute to the culture, altering what impacts our emotional cores so deeply.

Later that night, the concert of one of the great male fado singers, along with acoustic string instruments, had me and many audience members tearing up. I didn't know many of the words, yet I felt moved by the vibrations of songs of love and loss. It was a wonderful experience, being so emotionally present, in a nonaggressive way, surrounded by so many people. I was grateful, even as a foreigner, to feel such an accepted sense of belonging.

In Portugal I've stayed on organic farms and in vineyards, drunk wine from wineries that have been producing since the 1500s, and stayed in a hotel with no signage, which embraced me in its spiritual, ethereal atmosphere. Once, journeying to the Algarve in the south to play on the beaches and in the water, I was walking in a small town of ancient whitewashed buildings, feeling as though I were in a sacred movie set, and there on a wall was a poster for a Zen fair! I couldn't believe it, so I took a photo and inquired about the event, held at a stunning hotel that used to be a monastery. The gentle person behind the desk said he was attending the fair later in the afternoon. He gave me directions and suggested I stop at a wonderful vegan café on the way.

I wandered through this fairy tale, and after about an hour of happily getting lost, I came upon an elderly couple chatting with a younger man from Ireland. I inquired about the fair, and they smiled, saying, "Sit down and have a drink."

I obliged and we chatted. They let me know they lived across the road from the fairground and would drive me there soon. In the agricultural fairground were booths and workshops ranging from yoga to vegetarian eating to Reiki and massage. I befriended a young woman who had recently moved from England and was setting up a yoga center and school. She told me her practice was growing in the village. She had found an openness among the local folk generally not seen in small rural towns in Europe.

The spirit of this woman, and of so many of the people I've met in Portugal, still fills me with gratitude. And that gratitude comes from not feeling the need to dominate everything I encounter— and from other people not trying to dominate me. Being free to wander and learn and connect speaks much more to me of the beauty and meaning of life, and my worth as a person, than the superficial impressions we form when trying to further our base ambitions and fostering a competitive, conquering spirit.

Although I certainly feel different when I'm back in the United States, I still can find that gratitude here. On Friday nights in my home, I take the Sabbath time that Heschel talks about. I separate holy time from the profane, knowing that this will carry me through the week. I make the time to do it every week, not just once a year, because it is a reminder, and because I am human. Because I do fall out of balance living my life at various levels of extremes, often oblivious to what is really important. So, to court balance, I deliberately create a habit, a pattern, of coming back to that middle path, to that place of being fully present and grateful for the simple privilege of being alive with others in this world.

Every Friday evening, my family and I made a special meal together. We set the stage by lighting particular candles, knowing that we were bringing light into our home and into our hearts on that evening and that the light would stay with us the entire evening. In Jewish homes, there is a tradition that on Friday nights each one of us lights candles, including the youngest, to bring in the light. We played with sharing this blessing and the many ways light comes into our lives. We spoke and created prayers to bless this life, and we blessed each other. We blessed the creative intelligence that brought us together and asked us to share and engage in the abundance of light.

Jewish mystics tell a wonderful story about the beginning of time, when all was undifferentiated, and existence was only chaos. God was thinking of bringing light and knew that too much light was more than the human could actually handle, so God gave each of us a piece of it to hold.

Isn't that a wonderful thought: being blessed with the gift of life? The greatest aspect of holding that life is the blessing of discovering it in one another. That is the journey in life—finding the clues that will bring us home. We share a glass of wine together and a blessing that we can actually be with each other in this gift of the grapes of the vine and the nourishment that comes through it. We break bread together and make a blessing, thanking the universe for this sustenance that we are given. We then generally share a story or we read from a book that opens up the subject of gratitude for us to consider and reflect on and discuss. The stories are universal.

In my home, when I gathered with family, one week we would read from *Siddhartha;* another week we might read from early Jewish stories, maybe from the Zohar, the Mystical Books. We also would read from Quaker literature, always with the idea of bringing gratefulness more profoundly to our attention.

We'd share a meal that became a ritual, ancient and yet our own, in that the foods were traditional Friday-night foods. We'd look forward to the ritual as well as to sharing the blessings around the table. The conversation that stayed with us for the entire evening of bliss and brought us together as a family and community (we invited people to come to the table) was positive and uplifting and enveloping. No one had to direct the conversation. On those evenings, we were simply grateful, paying homage to the gift of this life.

Bringing ritual into our lives gives order and meaning. Ritual, if conducted with mindful attention, is also something we create together, and to do so, we can borrow from many traditions. We can create something that looks new. I learned much from sharing this ritual with my family, and, particularly through my stepson, who was nine at the time, I realized the purpose of having ordered rituals throughout our days. As an adult, so often I forget and just go about the busy habits of my day. We need to remember to listen to wherever the teachings are coming from—many times they come from the youth.

Now, years later, on Fridays I still acknowledge that it's the Sabbath, though it looks a little different, as I live alone. I still take personal time and move with a deliberately different rhythm, consciously making a choice as to who I want to be with and who I want to be. Also, I know Shabbat isn't limited to Fridays.

I urge you to give yourself Shabbat, Sabbath, retreat—whatever you call it and whenever you can call it in. This is the way we build ourselves lighthouses so that we can still see ourselves and the abundance in our lives even when we feel far away from shore. Sometimes I go out for a meal with a friend to a Vietnamese restaurant run by Buddhist nuns. The food is beautiful and the atmosphere peaceful, allowing me to drop into Shabbat. When I go there with one of my fellow students in my spiritual direction class, we're having Shabbat.

I choose to count my blessings. I make that perspective the brick and mortar of my foundation in life that I use to answer the tougher questions. In the circle of Shabbat, I can show up fully as myself and fully connected, and in that wholeness, I can find my way home.

PRACTICE

Focus on the previous questions of what you feel you deserve.

Now shift the question. What are you worth? Value and gratitude culminate not from the belief of what you should be given, but from the realization of what you can achieve and what you can give. The clearest path to knowing what you are worth is THROUGH giving. No matter how bad the place you are in currently feels, there is always a way to move beyond it.

This week, I want you to give. Find someone who needs you, or a cause that deserves your time, and show up. I don't mean "give till it hurts," as the saying goes. I want you to shoot past that idea and give until it DOESN'T hurt. Learn to make time and space, to count your blessings, and remind yourself that life is a gift.

Cultivate hope and let yourself feel awe of the amazing potential life offers us. Then you will experience gratitude. Then you will feel your foundation begin to shift into something that can sustain you. Once you have shifted and healed your perception of the world more realistically, you will make great strides in your path toward healing.

Home

Going home
Without my burden,
Going home
Behind the curtain,
Going home
Without the costume
That I wore…

LEONARD COHEN

HOME

Take me in
And hold me close,
For in my lonely place
I feel broken
And filled with pain.
I want to know I am whole again,
So soften my heart
To let you in,
Longing for love
And saying goodbye to fear.
Amen.

We have arrived home. What is home? Where is it? Home is the collective total of all the other qualities we have studied and enacted. Home is full circle, the beginning and end of the healing journey. It's also in the middle. Home is the spiritual inner-heart place where we can surrender to balance and be whole. Home encompasses all the other qualities; it is the vessel that holds them, starting with *reclaiming*.

Ultimately, home is the essential paradigm shift that allows us to exist in harmony with life, realizing that we provide the circuit between the natural world and the divine. Home is not like a drug that distracts us from our purpose or like a material object that can be bought or sold or taken to the grave. By "coming home" I mean welcoming the liberation of the heart and the full habitation and empowered presence of our lives.

Too many of us experience our days from someplace outside of our true selves, rather than being fully present and at home in our own skin. We split off from the most real aspects of ourselves in the false belief that we have to conform to the world. You know now that is not true. No more changing and separating yourself to meet the expectations of a false world. Make it the adventure of your life to create a world that is a home for your Stranger. I've learned that by using, learning, relearning, and reapplying the practices in this book and in our workshops, we can awaken at any moment and choose to embrace the gift of life. We can transcend circumstance and rise above the turmoil from a foundation of serenity.

We made an important journey to discover this place called home. The journey requires thinking about complicated questions, as I discovered in one of the groups I led. I particularly keyed into this as we created our spiritual autobiographies. One of the early reflective questions I asked was, "Where in your childhood home was your safe place?"

Rather quickly, one woman expressed anger and another cried, and they both let me know clearly that the question itself needed reframing. Neither had experienced a safe place in their childhood homes; for one, her safe place involved a deeply private part of her story, and the other had sought peace away from the home, under the canopy of a tree down the road. This workshop was an early reminder of how, during times when we cannot find solace in the environment we have been offered, we must expand our scope.

I reframed the question for future workshops. Instead I asked, "Where did you go that was a safe place as a child?" I encouraged participants to consider home as less of a physical structure and more like a sacred vessel.

Home is where we return to for healing, balance, and well-being. Home is wherever and whenever we give ourselves the gift of Shabbat, moving from ordinary to liminal time, and create our sanctuary within. This is how we respond to the messages the world gives us, trying to confuse us on our journey.

Throughout this journey home, I've suggested how to make small shifts, changes, and modifications to better inform the whole; I've talked about identifying our real priorities so that we can move into deeper truths about ourselves and each other. We started with evaluating our perspectives and attempting better self-awareness by filtering out the mixed messages we receive. We learned to shift focus inward, starting with our breath.

Breathing is the intimate key to our place of calm, our point of entry to wonder and magic. The invitation has been waiting for us all along, and the table of life is bountiful, but it can also be scary. But we have learned to welcome transition and the bounty it provides. A great journey starts with a breath, a step, and intention.

Whatever clarity you accomplish through this book, don't rest there. Keep challenging yourself; keep moving forward. We create a place for liminal time that takes us away from the illusions and anxiety of this place. That is our true home, where we come from, where we return, and where we can go to renew ourselves and meet ourselves again.

Although my heart is still wounded, I hold the ghosts of those injuries less tightly now, more often speaking with them and trying to heal them from the quiet, tender places my Stranger guides me to. I choose to have a permeable pericardium, as my friend once said, to keep my heart open and my boundaries pervious, to listen to wisdom as it gently guides me through thorns and thickets. I choose not to close but to open doors to my home, inviting other hearts searching for I-Thou to join me from their own quiet places.

It takes courage and acts of courage to request and find quiet, and also to reach out from there. Even our religious services give us other people's words through holy books, stories, and sermons. But we can feel uprooted and lost listening to other people's and institution's stories, and that is why we must make time and space to listen to our own stories.

Now I've created a space so I can enter my portal when I need or choose to. I needed to give myself this place, where I could welcome the gift, see the gift, and go in with my adult self or with my seven-year-old self. I know I need liminal time, and that I must set aside ordinary time for Shabbat and healing.

A healing place is a place of gentle ease, but to find it, you must take on the reclaiming work of looking into dark corners and engaging rather than tiptoeing. At times, I feel I hold a key to the front door, yet it won't turn. I forget to pay attention, to listen to my inner knowing, to enter my life clearly, with an open heart. In the quiet of my understanding, I realize the key is having an open heart with clarity—so that I both know and love the self I bring with me. When we try to enter through another doorway, hiding from our true story, there is always a cost—we are shut out from our home, and our Stranger cannot speak to us. To regain ourselves, we must return to that quiet place and let ourselves be led to action from our center, our core.

When we cultivate this cycle of balance and harmony between our desires, actions, and priorities, we can stand tall on the sometimes harrowing journey, and we come home with gratitude. We are grateful for arriving from the diaspora to home, because we know it's gratefulness that guides and moves us forward from our center of power.

When I lived in Australia, many years ago, I went to a play that brought me to tears. It was called *Yibiyung*, written by playwright Dallas Winmar. It tells the story of a girl, Yibiyung, who was taken from her family because she was of mixed aboriginal and white blood. Yibiyung stands in darkness beneath a tree, and her older self looks back and wonders aloud how she ended up at "this place."

We don't yet know where she means. She talks about understanding the time she was born into and the implication of the laws of that time in every aspect of her life, all against her will. She had no rights; everything was predetermined before she was even born. To have mixed blood was to fit nowhere, like a piece from a different puzzle shoved in the wrong box.

I love Yibiyung. So should you. She yearned for home so ardently that she ran away, refusing the name the state had given her and the number they defined her by. She was hunted like an outlaw until she found her way home, to her grandmother, and shared the story in the play. Yibiyung knew her worth and refused to give up in the face of what the world tried to force her to believe. Even on the run, she turned to her Stranger and to the home within herself to carry her all those desperate miles beyond oppression. Can we do less and call this a real life?

Now I'm learning to believe in myself again. Renew myself, again. Meet my Stranger again, always new, always in bloom. I listen to a voice that was silenced for what felt like forever. I am ready to continue my journey from places I thought were home, in my mind or physicality, to muster up the *ruach*, the Hebrew spirit, the wind of all the galaxies, and say yes.

I still believe in wishing upon a star. I always need to remind myself that I have a piece of that light within me, the light that loves and honors me and keeps me alive. The mystic story that says we hold as much as we can handle at each moment is not a fable. The light glows brighter when we open up for more to shine. Coming home is like finding the porch light on, a beacon shining with our own personal light frequency, showing us the right path. I had my eyes open, yet I was looking peripherally rather than straight ahead.

Arriving home for me means going ever deeper into my heart and learning to take things in through my heart, to my mind, and then allowing the impulses to be sent out through my body, out into the world. I like listening through my heart, as well as the continuing practice and work it requires of me.

First I have to come to peace with myself. I find my light in the portal, sitting by the pond under the willow, pen in hand, listening to guidance, a sacred gift. Huffing and puffing, I invite grace to the table, gently, when I am quiet enough to listen with intention. I find my light, and I find myself. I make myself a perennial home, which I carry with me.

As I have said, there is no microwavable solution to the problems of this world; you can't just stick this book, for example, in the machine and wait till you hear the "ding" of inner contentment. I believe you should find your own mantras, your own path, your own journey, and there are no easy solutions. It takes every step you took to escape to bring you back home.

My friends, life will still happen. You will trip. People will disappoint you. You will disappoint others. You will disappoint yourself—maybe even more so now that you're rebuilding your foundation according to new standards and living with eyes wide open. You don't meditate once and gain enlightenment. You keep living, you keep moving, you become the messenger. You own your mistakes, and now you are excited about what you can learn from them.

You are awake, you are aware, you are intentional. You have learned to tune in to your resistance. You now welcome it, right? Keep acting like you do, and one day you'll be surprised that you really do. I like to think of the age-old fable of the tortoise and the hare. Society desperately wants you to be the hare, running for its dollars and burning out. Alternatively, be the tortoise. Yes, the hare runs faster in his ever-frenzied state, but the finish line eludes him. The tortoise is always home already, proceeding in peace. He goes where his journey takes him, carrying his home with him. He is grounded.

I could drop dead any moment, and so could you. Ignoring that fact doesn't make the idea any less stressful. What makes the idea of mortality manageable is living your life the best you can with confidence, purpose, and the joy of transcendent connection. Otherwise, you'll be misplaced for that minute or for another hundred years; what does it matter? Claim your peace NOW. Be your best self NOW.

When you carry our Stranger with you, you are home. Life is no longer a collection of specific yet random tasks. Life is no longer an insipid rerun pockmarked with endless commercial breaks. You are no longer in survival mode. You are no longer dissociated. You are awake, you are breathing, you are both connected and free. You are free and you are home!

Another thought I want to return to is not to let your childhood be your soul's high-water mark. Don't accept a descent from your own purity. Continue the journey your childhood promised you when the world felt huge and we all felt connected. Those times—even if they were too few—when love was easy and when you were fearless. Become those things again. Be fearless now. If you have the courage to be your own hero, you will always be at home on your soul's path, where you can bloom brightly.

I suppose the irony is that I am talking about a journey where you arrive back where you started. Ideally, you now find peace within, where the journey starts and ends. All the real change happens within, and, since it's not a race, there's no scorecard, no way to measure your progress or count how many miles you've logged. But if this were a video game, you would have a million points by now for all the work you've done! *You* are the master! You are ready to move forward. Always, home offers an open invitation, and just like Dorothy, who missed home so much, we are all on a journey, for the most powerful reason: being fully present in life. Sometimes it takes a storm to make us realize how far from home we are.

Heed your inner path. Love your Stranger. Your Stranger is the love within you, and no one will ever know you better or love you more deeply. Find the right friends to travel with, and you will find the faith to return home. Just remember, especially when the journey is hard and the night is long, "There's no place like home, there's no place like home..."

And right now, in this beautiful moment, here you are. *Take a breath.*

About Arnie

Arnie Freiman is a lot of things—a certified spiritual director, an innovator in health and wellness solutions, a certified financial planner, a PhD, and an ordained chaplain. He's a father, a cancer survivor, and an ex-husband, too. Heck, he's even a poet. He was one of the earliest people to introduce holistic health education at a major national university, and he co-founded the first acupuncture school in the United States and founded the first naturopathic college in California. So he's been around. He's done extraordinary things, and he's held many titles. His favorite is Friend, a moniker he values over all others.

For information about booking Arnie to speak at your event, please contact:
Arnie Freiman
arnie@arniefreiman.com
arniefreiman.com
@arniefreiman